THE MOST VALUABLE CORPORATE FORMS YOU'LL EVER NEED

THE MOST VALUABLE CORPORATE FORMS YOU'LL EVER NEED

James C. Ray
Attorney at Law

Sphinx Publishing
A Division of Sourcebooks, Inc.
Naperville, IL • Clearwater, FL

Second Edition, 1998

Published by: **Sphinx® Publishing, A Division of Sourcebooks, Inc.**

Naperville Office	Clearwater Office
P.O. Box 372	P.O. Box 25
Naperville, Illinois 60566	Clearwater, Florida 33757
(630) 961-3900	(813) 587-0999
FAX: 630-961-2168	FAX: 813-586-5088

Cover Design: Andrew Sardina/Dominique Raccah, Sourcebooks, Inc.
Interior Design and Production: Andrew Sardina, Sourcebooks, Inc.

This publication is designed to provide accurate and authoritative information in regard to the subject matter covered. It is sold with the understanding that the publisher is not engaged in rendering legal, accounting, or other professional service. If legal advice or other expert assistance is required, the services of a competent professional person should be sought.

From a Declaration of Principles Jointly Adopted by a Committee of the
American Bar Association and a Committee of Publishers and Associations

Library of Congress Cataloging-in-Publication Data
Ray, James C.
      The most valuable corporate forms you'll ever need / James C. Ray.
   —2nd ed.
         p.   cm.
Includes index.
      ISBN 1-57071-346-4 (pbk.)
      1. Corporation law—United States—Forms. 2. Corporation law—
United States—Popular works.   I. Title.
KF1411.R39   1998
346.73'066'0269—dc21   98-6006
                                                                                                          CIP

Printed and bound in the United States of America.

Paperback — 10 9 8 7 6 5 4 3 2

CONTENTS

Using Self-Help Law Books

Whenever you shop for a product or service, you are faced with various levels of quality and price. In deciding what product or service to buy, you make a cost/value analysis on the basis of your willingness to pay and the quality you desire.

When buying a car, you decide whether you want transportation, comfort, status, or sex appeal. Accordingly, you decide among such choices as a Neon, a Lincoln, a Rolls Royce, or a Porsche. Before making a decision, you usually weigh the merits of each option against the cost.

When you get a headache, you can take a pain reliever (such as aspirin) or visit a medical specialist for a neurological examination. Given this choice, most people, of course, take a pain reliever, since it costs only pennies, whereas a medical examination costs hundreds of dollars and takes a lot of time. This is usually a logical choice because rarely is anything more than a pain reliever needed for a headache. But in some cases, a headache may indicate a brain tumor, and failing to see a specialist right away can result in complications. Should everyone with a headache go to a specialist? Of course not, but people treating their own illnesses must realize that they are betting on the basis of their cost/value analysis of the situation, they are taking the most logical option.

The same cost/value analysis must be made in deciding to do one's own legal work. Many legal situations are very straight forward, requiring a simple form and no complicated analysis. Anyone with a little intelligence and a book of instructions can handle the matter without outside help.

But there is always the chance that complications are involved that only an attorney would notice. To simplify the law into a book like this, several legal cases often must be condensed into a single sentence or paragraph. Otherwise, the book would be several hundred pages long and too complicated for most people. However, this simplification necessarily leaves out many details and nuances that would apply to special or unusual situations. Also, there are many ways to interpret most legal questions. Your case may come before a judge who disagrees with the analysis of our authors.

Therefore, in deciding to use a self-help law book and to do your own legal work, you must realize that you are making a cost/value analysis and deciding that the chance your case will not turn out to your satisfaction is outweighed by the money you will save in doing it yourself. Most people handling their own simple legal matters never have a problem, but occasionally people find that it ended up costing them more to have an attorney straighten out the situation than it would have if they had hired an attorney in the beginning. Keep this in mind while handling your case, and be sure to consult an attorney if you feel you might need further guidance.

Introduction

Purpose of This Book

It is hoped that using this book will save you some legal fees. It may even be that using this book will save you having to hire a lawyer at some time, but that is not its purpose. It has three purposes. First is to help you manage and organize your corporation so as to make the occasions on which you need a lawyer as few as possible. Second is to help you recognize the occasions on which a lawyer's advice is essential. Third is to more efficiently use the lawyer you hire.

Failing to hire a lawyer when you need one is not likely to save you money. If, in reading this book, you discover that what you want to do involves more complications than you imagined, or if what you want to do involves a large sum of money, then get a lawyer. If all goes well, you can complain about paying for something you didn't need after all. That's better than not hiring a lawyer and having something more serious to complain about.

Some clients believe that, having turned a matter over to the lawyers, they are released from all further responsibility. "After all," such a client thinks, "if I pay a large amount of money for my lawyer to draft a contract, why should I bore myself by reading it. It's the lawyer's job to make sure it's right."

But that makes the lawyer's job nearly impossible. You know your business and what is important for it. The best lawyer's ideas about that may be completely wrong, and he or she may attach importance to the unimportant (because it was important to the last client) and gloss over a critical factor. Use this book to know what to expect from your lawyer and why. And then read and understand the work your lawyer does for you. Make sure it works for you.

ORGANIZATION OF THIS BOOK

This book deals with governing the corporation—corporate decision-making by shareholders and directors, and management by officers. This will help you organize decision making and record keeping, some of which you can do better than a lawyer could. This book is not about how you operate your business in dealing with the outside world. For forms to operate your business, Sourcebooks offers *The Most Valuable Business Forms You'll Ever Need.*

The main text of this book explains the various types of resolutions and other forms typically used in governing a business. Sample forms are contained throughout the text. These are examples for an imaginary corporation to give you some idea of how your finished forms should look.

Rather than include a resolution for every conceivable use, blank resolution forms are included in appendix B, and the important language is included in the text. This language may need to be adapted for your specific situation. Each resolution in the main part of the book is surrounded by a double box (☐), and is given and letter and number designation (R-1, R-2, etc.). In each resolution you will see certain words that are both highlighted and in brackets. This indicates a space to fill in certain information, and what information needs to be inserted. For example, resolution R-18, on page 74, reads as follows:

R-18. **Provision of articles of incorporation establishing a class of preferred shares—** `Article [article number]. The number of shares the corporation is authorized to issue is` **[total number of shares authorized]** `which shall be divided into two classes as follows:`

Class	Series	Par value	Number of shares
[Common/Preferred]	**[if any]**	**[No par/amount]**	**[number of shares]**

`The preferences, limitations and relative rights of each class and series of preferred shares shall be as determined by the board of directors pursuant to` **[your state's version of MBCA, Sec. 6.02]** `before the issuance of any shares of that class and series.`

If your corporation was operating under the laws of Florida, your version of this resolution (which would be inserted in either Form 5, 6, 8, or 10) might look like this (the filled-in information in the example below is highlighted for easier reference to the form above):

`Article` **8.** `The number of shares the corporation is authorized to issue is` **200,000** `which shall be divided into two classes as follows:`

Class	Series	Par value	Number of shares
Common		**No par**	100,000
Preferred	**A**	**No par**	100,000

`The preferences, limitations and relative rights of each class and series of preferred shares shall be as determined by the board of directors pursuant to` **Florida Statutes, Sec. 607.0602,** `before the issuance of any shares of that class and series.`

Appendix A is a list of the corporation statutes for each state. This will tell you where to look for more information. You should be familiar with your state's corporation statute and keep a copy on hand. Often it provides specific rules you must follow to operate legally.

Appendix B contains the blank forms you can use. Some of these forms will require you to fill in information by referring to the various resolutions in the main part of the book. To help you with this, there is a table on page 9. Many of the forms are resolutions for adoption by the shareholders or directors, to be combined into minutes of meetings, consents of action, or separate resolution forms which are explained and illustrated in chapter 1.

The forms are intentionally simple in style. Some of them may be more simple than real life applications will allow, but the basics are here.

HOW TO USE THE FORMS

To give you a good overview of governing your corporation, it is suggested that you first read through this entire book. Then, by using the table of contents, the table of forms, or the index, locate the section of the text which explains the form you need. This will refer you to a blank form in appendix B. If you are dealing with one of the resolutions, you will use Form 9 (for board of director resolutions) or Form 10 (for shareholder resolutions). Next insert the data called for in the form. In some cases this will be a few names, in others you will need to insert a lengthy resolution. You can either photocopy the blank forms and type on them, or retype the entire forms.

There are no references to specific statutes. This book is intended to be used by people all over the country, so no specific statute is relevant to every reader. There are a few mentions of the Revised Model Business Corporation Act of 1984 which is referred to in the text as the Model Business Corporation Act or the "MBCA." The purpose of such references is to help you find your way in the statutes of your state. Many states have adopted the MBCA with variations. (There is a directory of state business corporation statutes in appendix A of this book.) If yours is one of them, the MBCA reference will look something like the citation for the corresponding provision in your state statute. For example, Section 1.40 of the MBCA is found in the North Carolina Business Corporation Act, found at North Carolina General Statutes, section 55-1-40. (This is abbreviated as "N.C.G.S., §55-1-40." If you look this up you will find it in books titled "The General Statutes of North Carolina," but they are commonly, and officially, referred to as "North Carolina General Statutes." Apparently either the lawyers and judges of North Carolina, or the Michie Company which publishes the books, don't know the proper title.)

TABLE OF FORMS

The following list of forms will help you to locate, and put together, the forms you need. These forms are located in appendix B of this book.

Forms 9 and 10 will be used in a different manner from the other forms. If you look at Form 9 in appendix B, you will see that it is a blank form for a resolution of the board of directors. To create forms 9.01 through 9.48, you need to look up the particular resolution in the main part of the book, and insert that language in the blank space in Form 9. In the listing below for forms 9.01 through 9.48, the abbreviation "DR" stands for "Directors' Resolution." After the description of each resolution you will see a reference such as "[R-1]." This means, go to resolution R-1 in the main part of this book, and insert that language in Form 9 from appendix B. The page number given below will tell you where to find that particular resolution. For example, Form 9.12 is a Directors' Resolution (DR) which relates to issuing stock. To create this form, you would take the language from Resolution-15 [R-15] on page 63, and type that language in the blank space on Form 9. Apply these same instructions to Form 10 and forms 10.01 through 10.23, which relate to Shareholders' Resolutions (SR).

The resolutions listed as either "director" or "shareholder" are those more commonly made be each group, however, you are not necessarily limited by the designations. Some of those designated as director resolutions may also be made by your shareholders. And, if permitted by your corporation's articles or bylaws, some of those designated as shareholder resolutions may also be made by the directors. If either of these situations apply to your corporation, you can insert the appropriate resolution language in either Form 9 or Form 10.

Remember that resolutions are adopted by either the board of directors or the shareholders. This means they must be used along with either form 1, 2, 4, 5, 6, or 8. You have two options for how to issue resolutions. First, you can simply type the resolution on the appropriate form for the minutes (i.e., form 1, 2, 4, 5, 6, or 8). In this case, you will not need to use Form 9 or Form 10. The second option is to type each resolution on either Form 9 or Form 10. In this case, you would check the box on the form for the minutes which reads: "See attached resolutions." You would then staple the resolutions to the minutes.

The following forms is a list of forms:

CORPORATE DECISION MAKING 1

MEETINGS AND ADOPTION OF RESOLUTIONS

Corporations are "people" too. When an individual makes a decision, it's a pretty simple matter. Suppose you're thinking about a new car. You may need advice, and you may need to think about it a long time, but when the time comes to make the decision, it's a mental snap of the fingers. When you put your name on the dotted line at the dealership, that's all the evidence needed that the decision is made.

Under the law, corporations are "persons," but they are only imaginary creations. They can make decisions like other persons, but how do you know when an imaginary person has made a decision, and how do you prove it? Corporations have a legal existence, but, like puppets, they only act and move when their shareholders, officers and directors give them life. They only do what we say they do, nothing more and nothing less. Since a corporation is a collective body, that is, made up of the separate individuals who are its shareholders, officers and directors, a corporation can only make a collective decision, and collective decisions are made in meetings of one kind or another.

Since a corporation is separate from the collection of individuals who own and manage it, there must be some form of communication between it and its masters. This separation is extremely important, because without it, the corporation may for some purposes cease to exist. If a corporation's owner runs the corporation's business in a way that makes it inseparable from his or her existence as an individual, then under the legal doctrine known as *piercing the corporate veil* a court may ignore the corporation altogether. The result may be that a plaintiff or creditor can satisfy a judgment out of the owner's personal assets rather than the corporation's. One of the ways you maintain this critical separation is to keep the formal lines of communication between the corporation and its owners and directors open, healthy and operating. The proof of this separation is in the care with which you call and conduct shareholders' and directors' meetings and, particularly, the way you record the decisions made in the meetings. (Of course there are other important steps to take in avoiding piercing the corporate veil. For example, make sure you keep the corporation's bank account and other assets separate from your personal business.)

Proving it. When you went into the car dealer's office and put your signature on the contract to buy a car, the salesperson didn't need to ask, "How do I know you really intend to be bound by this contract?" You were there in person, and the dealer could see that you yourself signed it. A corporation can't do that. Not being an individual, a corporation can't sign its own name; it must act through an agent. If you sent your next door neighbor to buy the car for you, and your neighbor signed your name on the line, the salesperson certainly would ask that question, and your neighbor would have to show some kind of proof of authority.

A corporation has the same problem. How would you go about proving that the corporation really wants a new car and that it's agent, usually an officer, really has the power to sign the company's name on the contract? The proof can only be found in the written record of the decision making process. A corporation "decides" when its shareholders or directors meet to make collective decisions, and, because the corporation can't speak for itself, the outside world learns about the decision by having a look at the record.

FORMAL MINUTES

One of the primary records is the "minutes" of corporate meetings. Minutes are basically a written summary of what occurs at meetings of the board of directors and meetings of the shareholders. Boards of directors usually have regularly scheduled meetings, such as weekly or monthly. Shareholders do not meet as often as the board, and typically only meet once a year. However, as important matters sometimes cannot wait for the next regular meeting, sometimes there is a need for special meetings of both the board and the shareholders.

In corporations with a large number of directors, smaller "committees" are sometimes formed as a more efficient way of conducting business. Form 1 or Form 2 can be adapted for committee meetings by simply designating the name of the committee after the name of the corporation (see page 20 for an example).

Appendix B includes forms for use for the various types of meetings. Space is provided on these forms to fill in the name of your corporation, other basic information, and whatever minutes apply to the particular meeting. Form 1 is to record minutes of a meeting of a regular meeting of the board of directors. Form 2 is for minutes of a special meeting of the board of directors, Form 5 for the annual shareholders meeting, and Form 6 for a special shareholders meeting.

On the following pages are examples of what the written record of three corporate decisions might look like. The first is from a special meeting of the shareholders (Form 6). The second is from a special meeting of the board of directors (Form 2). The third is from a special meeting of the "Executive Committee" of the board of directors (also using Form 2).

Minutes of a special shareholders meeting—

Minutes of Special Meeting of the Shareholders of

Scrupulous Corporation

A special meeting of the Shareholders of the Corporation was held on the date and at the time and place set forth in the written notice of meeting, or waiver of notice signed by shareholders, and attached to the minutes of this meeting.

The following shareholders were present:

Shareholder	No. of Shares
Henry Hardy	20,000
Raymond Rodriguez	15,000
Della Driskell	15,000
Calvin Collier	15,000
Hugh Hardy	20,000
Roberta Moore	15,000

The meeting was called to order and it was moved, seconded and carried that Raymond Rodriguez act as Chairman and that Roberta Moore act as Secretary.

A roll call was taken and the Chairman noted that all of the outstanding shares of the Corporation were represented in person or by proxy. Any proxies are attached to these minutes.

Minutes of the preceding meeting of the Shareholders, held on January 5, 1997, were read and approved.

Upon motion duly made, seconded and carried, the following resolution(s) was/were adopted:

The Chairman informed the shareholders that Mr. Henry Hardy, citing his advanced age, had resigned from the board of directors, effective July 9, 1997, and recommended that the shareholders act promptly to fill the vacancy created by his resignation. He then asked the shareholders for nominations for the position of director.

Mr. Calvin Collier nominated Ms. Della Driskell a shareholder who was present at the meeting. There were no additional nominations, and Ms. Driskell was elected by the unanimous vote of the shareholders to serve as director of the corporation to complete Mr. Hardy's term and until her successor is elected and qualified.

There being no further business, the meeting adjourned.

Roberta Moore
Secretary

Approved:

Raymond Rodriguez

Minutes of a special directors meeting—

Minutes of Special Meeting of the Board of Directors of

Scrupulous Corporation

A special meeting of the Board of Directors of the Corporation was held on the date and at the time and place set forth in the written notice of meeting, or waiver of notice signed by directors, and attached to the minutes of this meeting.

The following directors were present: Della Driskell, Roberta Moore, Raymond Rodriguez, and Calvin Collier.

The meeting was called to order and it was moved, seconded and carried that Raymond Rodriguez act as Chairman and that Roberta Moore act as Secretary.

Minutes of the preceding meeting of the Board, held on January 9, 1997, were read and approved.

Upon motion duly made, seconded and carried, the following resolution(s) was/were adopted:

The Chairman called the meeting to order at 10:45 a.m. He then asked the President to present a report.

The President reported on the need of a delivery vehicle for the company's use.

Mr. Hardy moved the adoption of the following resolution which, after discussion, was duly adopted by the unanimous vote of the Directors:

RESOLVED, that the Corporation shall purchase an automobile at a cost of not more that $18,000 which, in the opinion of the President of the corporation, shall be suitable for making deliveries to customers.

FURTHER RESOLVED, that the President or his designees are authorized and directed to negotiate such purchase for the corporation and to execute such contracts or other documents as may be necessary or desirable to complete the purchase.

There being no further business, the meeting adjourned.

Roberta Moore
Secretary

Approved:

Raymond Rodriguez

Minutes of a special committee meeting—

Minutes of Special Meeting of the Board of Directors of

Scrupulous Corporation (Executive Committee)

A special meeting of the Board of Directors of the Corporation was held on the date and at the time and place set forth in the written notice of meeting, or waiver of notice signed by directors, and attached to the minutes of this meeting.

The following directors were present: Della Driskell, Roberta Moore, Raymond Rodriguez, and Calvin Collier .

The meeting was called to order and it was moved, seconded and carried that Raymond Rodriguez act as Chairman and that Roberta Moore act as Secretary.

Minutes of the preceding meeting of the Board, held on January 9, 1997 , were read and approved.

Upon motion duly made, seconded and carried, the following resolution(s) was/were adopted:

The President reported on progress in negotiating the purchase of a new delivery vehicle as authorized by the Directors on July 10, 1997. He informed the Committee that, in his opinion, rather than purchasing a car as had been discussed in such meeting, it would be to the company's advantage to purchase a small van that would carry a larger load and allow more efficient deliveries. Such a van, he said, could be purchased for $18,000, the amount authorized in the Directors' original resolution. Since the directors' authorization had specified the purchase of an automobile, the President thought it necessary to seek the Committee's advice on whether it would be appropriate to purchase the van instead.

Ms. Driskell moved the adoption of the following resolution which, after brief discussion, was adopted by the unanimous vote of the members of the committee.

RESOLVED, that the purchase of a delivery van, shall be deemed to be consistent with the Directors' intent in adopting its resolution on July 10, 1997, and the President is therefore authorized to proceed with the purchase of a van at a cost of not more than $18,000.

There being no further business, the meeting adjourned.

Roberta Moore
Secretary

Approved:

Raymond Rodriguez

Running a business requires hundreds of decisions. Of course, not all of them are important enough to command the attention of the directors or shareholders, but many do. The business corporation statutes of the various states usually allow another method of making corporate decisions which can greatly reduce the expense and inconvenience of frequent meetings. A "consent to action without formal meeting" may be very useful when a needed decision can be reached without a face to face discussion. It is particularly helpful when the decision makers are scattered and can't meet without expensive and time-consuming travel.

Most states require that, in order to be effective, consents to action or "written consents" must be in writing and signed (consented to) by all the shareholders or directors entitled to vote. That requirement means that a company with a large number of shareholders won't reasonably be able to use this method. You'd never be able to collect the large number of signatures needed. However, for most boards of directors and directors' committees, and for the shareholders of some small corporations, it is a very useful device indeed. Also, for those small corporations with only one director or shareholder, written consents avoid the awkward feeling of one person having a "meeting" all alone. Form 4 is for the directors' consent, and Form 8 for the shareholders' consent. Spaces are provided to fill in the name of your corporation and the details of what action is being approved. On the following page you will find two examples:

Consent to action without a meeting by directors—

Consent to Action Without Formal Meeting of Directors of

Scrupulous Corporation

The undersigned, being all of the Directors of the Corporation, hereby adopt the following resolutions:

WHEREAS, the President of the corporation has reported on the need of the corporation for an automobile for use in making deliveries to the company's customers and the directors have concluded that it is in the interest of the corporation to purchase an automobile for the purposes described in the President's report, it is therefore

RESOLVED, that the Corporation shall purchase an automobile at a cost of not more that $18,000 which, in the opinion of the President of the corporation, shall be suitable for making deliveries.

FURTHER RESOLVED, that the President or his designees are authorized and directed to negotiate such purchase for the corporation and to execute such contracts or other documents as may be necessary or desirable to complete the purchase.

RESOLVED, that these resolutions shall be effective at _____ 11:00 _____ a .m., on _____ July 10 _____, _____ 1997 _____.

Raymond Rodriguez		*Della Driskell*	
Raymond Rodriguez,	Director	Della Driskell,	Director
Calvin Collier		*Roberta Moore*	
Calvin Collier,	Director	Roberta Moore,	Director

Consent to action without a meeting by shareholders—

Consent to Action Without Formal Meeting of Shareholders of

Scrupulous Corporation

The undersigned, being all of the shareholders of the Corporation, hereby adopt the following resolutions:

WHEREAS, Mr. Henry Hardy, citing his advanced age, has resigned from the board of directors of the corporation, effective July 9, 1997, thereby creating a vacancy on the board of directors, and WHEREAS, it is the wish of the shareholders to fill the vacancy promptly, it is therefore

RESOLVED, that Ms. Della Driskell is hereby elected to serve as director of the corporation to complete the remainder of Mr. Hardy's term and until her successor is elected and qualified, and

RESOLVED, that these resolutions shall be effective at _____ 10:00 _____ a .m., on _____ July 19 _____, _____ 1997 _____.

Henry Hardy		*Raymond Rodriguez*	
Henry Hardy,	Shareholder	Raymond Rodriguez,	Shareholder
Della Driskell		*Calvin Collier*	
Della Driskell,	Shareholder	Calvin Collier,	Shareholder
Hugh Hardy		*Roberta Moore*	
Hugh Hardy,	Shareholder	Roberta Moore,	Shareholder

MINUTE BOOKS—THE CORPORATE MEMORY

What are minute books for? The corporate minute books are the log books or the diary of a corporation. Most of us are perfectly able to get through our lives without keeping a diary, but there are times when we all wish we had one. Quickly now, can you think what year you moved into your present house? When was it you took the summer vacation in the mountains?

At least we have our memories to rely on, however faulty. A corporation has no useful memory unless we give it one. If it relies on the various memories of its shareholders, officers and directors, it will have as many conflicting memories as it does shareholders, officers and directors, and such memories are notorious for fading or, worse yet, evolving to suit the purposes of the individuals trying to remember.

The minute books, then, are the official memory of the corporation. The persons who participate in management and decision making are responsible for agreeing on the official version of events and recording them. Once "approved," the official record is legally presumed to be the correct version of events, and anyone who would deny their accuracy (in a court of law, for example) has the burden of proving them inaccurate.

The minutes shouldn't be taken lightly; although, unfortunately, many times they are. How often have you heard meetings open with a statement from the chair to the effect that "unless there is objection, the chair will omit the reading of the minutes of the last meeting" or someone will "move that the minutes of the last meeting be approved without reading?" There's seldom any objection. But the formal "reading" is supposed to be for the purpose of approving the accuracy of the minutes of the previous meeting. A director who fails to review the old minutes and make objection to any inaccuracy he or she finds before the formal approval may regret it.

Who can look at the minutes? Don't imagine that the minutes of a directors or shareholders meeting will be kept secret. There are many times that good business will require the distribution of official *certified* copies of the minutes to outsiders (see Form 11 and Form 12), and times that a court or administrative agency (for example, the IRS) will subpoena minutes. Some closely regulated businesses must turn over the minutes to a regulatory agency as a matter of course. In many cases, the shareholders of a corporation may have a statutory right to look at the minutes of the directors meetings as well as the shareholder minutes. So when you put something down in the minute book, imagine it being read by the person you would least like to have read it. It could easily happen.

How to write the minutes. There are at least two schools of thought about this. Some say that the more detail you have, the better. If the purpose of the minutes is to show that the directors are doing a conscientious job and carefully giving lengthy consideration to each important issue to come before them, then detail is important. Following this line of reasoning, you would want the minutes to reflect the pros and cons and describe the vigorous give and take of the meeting. Suppose the board of directors decides to lead the corporation into a new line of business by acquiring a new subsidiary. It's a big investment, and a year later it proves to be a questionable one. An unhappy shareholder sues the directors for their careless management. The directors will want to defend themselves by showing that, although their decision may not have worked out well, they were far from careless and had made a well informed, reasonable business judgment. The directors will want to introduce into evidence the minutes of the meeting at which they made the decision to show the care with which they deliberated. If the minutes are complete and show a reasonable basis for the decision, it may make the difference in mounting a successful defense.

Others say too much detail in the minutes can be a dangerous practice. Suppose there is a heated debate about some issue, and one of the directors tells the rest that if they make a certain decision, "there will be hell to pay, and the corporation will be belly-up in a year." The majority disregards the warning and makes the decision. The secretary dutifully records the decision along with the dissenting director's warning. The decision quickly proves to be a bad one, and when the year is up, the company is in a bad way. A disgruntled shareholder sues the directors for their incompetent management and introduces the minutes into evidence at trial. The directors will look pretty bad. The minutes will show that they had fair warning from the wise dissenter that their decision was a foolish one. Score one for the plaintiff.

So detail in the minute books can be a two edged sword. There are legitimate reasons for taking a concise approach, stating the decisions made and noting dissenting views where the dissenting directors request it, and there are reasons for taking the detailed approach, demonstrating that the directors take their duties seriously, investigating all sides of each issue. There is no reason, however, for including details that can only prove embarrassing. If one director expresses the opinion that the other directors are insufferable twits, it's hard to imagine any future occasion on which it will be advantageous to have that remark on the record.

It can also be a mistake to be anything other than consistent in the approach taken. If the secretary fills page after page of the minute book with detailed reports of meetings, and then reports one meeting in uncharacteristic lack of detail, the comparison will beg the question, "What happened at this meeting that they're trying to hide?" Or, if the secretary usually writes minutes in a concise style, but for one meeting goes to unusual lengths in reporting detail, someone may want to know why and decide it warrants special investigation.

Forms 1, 2, 5 and 6 are to record minutes of your directors or shareholders meetings. Space is provided to fill in the name of your corporation, various standard provisions, and the minutes of the particular meeting. Use additional pages (Form 3 and Form 7 are continuation pages for minutes) and attach them to this form, if necessary.

Following are two reports of the same events showing two different styles of reporting minutes:

Minutes reporting discussion and vote on the purchase of real property (detailed form)—

Mr. Hugh Hardy, the chairman of the meeting then asked the President, Mr. Rodriguez, to present a report on the company's needs for additional office space.

Mr. Rodriguez noted that the offices presently occupied by the company had been purchased in 1974 when its employees had numbered fewer than fifty. Since that time, the staff had increased to more than one hundred, necessitating the crowding of two or more employees into spaces originally intended for only one. In addition, the company had been forced to rent temporary office space for the accounting division in another building which, although it was only a few miles away, nevertheless required frequent trips back and forth and complicated computer links and resulted in much waste of time and expense.

The company's present building, although in need of renovation, is in sound structural condition, Mr. Rodriguez reported, but not able to be expanded on the land presently owned by the company. However, it had recently been reported to management that the vacant land adjacent to the company building is available for purchase, and Mr. Rodriguez had approached its owners about purchasing the land with a view toward expanding the company headquarters.

Mr. Rodriguez reported that the asking price for the vacant lot is $150,000, but he thought he could negotiate the price down to as low as $135,000. He next presented to the meeting charts showing the comparative costs of (a) continuing operations as is, with the expectation that additional off premises space would need to be rented within the next 24 months, (b) selling the present building and building or renting space elsewhere capable of serving the entire operation, or (c) acquiring the adjacent lot and expanding the current facilities. The third option indicated savings of 20% and 15% over the cost of the first two respectively over a five year period. (The report presented by Mr. Rodriguez is filed in management storage file No. 94-56.)

Mr. Hugh Hardy commented that the most economical decision is not always the wisest, and wondered whether the erection of a new building might be desirable considering the public relations advantages of such a move. Mr. Rodriguez agreed that the public relations would be valuable, but believed that restoring and renovating the current headquarters would result in equally beneficial public notice and result in substantial savings as well.

Ms. Driskell questioned several specific assumptions underlying Mr. Rodriguez's report, and then announced her satisfaction with their reasonableness. She then moved the adoption of the following resolutions:

RESOLVED, that the President is authorized and directed to negotiate a contract for the purchase of the lot adjacent to the company's headquarters as described in his report (management storage file No. 94-56) for a cash purchase price of not more than $145,000.

FURTHER RESOLVED, that the officers of the corporation are authorized to execute such contract together with such other documents as may be necessary or desirable to complete the described purchase within 120 days of the date of this resolution.

Ms. Moore seconded the motion, and the Chairman asked whether there was any further discussion.

Ms. Moore asked Mr. Rodriguez whether 120 days would be sufficient to complete the purchase. Mr. Rodriguez replied that he believed the time was sufficient, but would anticipate that the board would grant an extension of the time if proved necessary. The consensus of the board was that reasonable extensions would be granted.

Mr. Henry Hardy objected to the purchase of the property for cash, believing it to place an unneeded burden on the company's cash position. He recommended that the acquisition be financed through a bank loan secured by a mortgage on the property. Mr. Rodriguez said that he expected to finance the building expansion with such a mortgage, as indicated in his comparison figures, but thought the transaction would be more expeditiously completed if the land were purchased for cash, and that a rapid completion of the purchase would be a strong negotiating point with the seller.

There being no further discussion, the chairman asked for a vote on the resolutions. The resolutions were adopted with four votes in favor. Mr. Henry Hardy voted against the resolutions and asked that his vote and his objection to the cash purchase arrangement be noted in these minutes.

Minutes reporting discussion and vote on the purchase of real property (concise form)—

Mr. Rodriguez next reported on the company's need for additional office space, explaining that the number of employees has expanded greatly since its present location was first occupied. A copy of the President's report is filed in management storage file No. 94-56. The directors noted that figures presented by Mr. Rodriguez in his report predicted that the company would gain substantial savings over a five year period by purchasing and expanding onto the vacant lot adjacent to the company's present location compared to the renting of additional needed space or relocation of the company's operation elsewhere.

The following resolutions, moved for adoption by Ms. Driskell, seconded by Ms. Moore, were adopted after discussion of the President's report.

RESOLVED, that the President is authorized and directed to negotiate a contract for the purchase of the lot adjacent to the company's headquarters as described in his report (management storage file No. 94-56) for a cash purchase price of not more than $145,000.

FURTHER RESOLVED, that the officers of the corporation are authorized to execute such contract together with such other documents as may be necessary or desirable to complete the described purchase within 120 days of the date of this resolution.

There were four votes in favor of adoption. Mr. Henry Hardy objected to the purchase of the property for cash rather than financing the purchase with a bank loan. He voted against adoption of the resolution, asking that his opposition be noted in these minutes.

An alternative to writing all of the resolutions in the minutes is to have a separate sheet for each resolution. Form 9 and Form 10 can be used for this purpose. These resolutions can then be attached to the minutes. The benefit is that it will later be easier for the secretary to simply copy the appropriate resolution and attach it to a certification statement (Form 11 or Form 12) if necessary; instead of having to search through the minutes to find the resolution, then re-writing it to certify.

How does an outsider know when a corporation has made a decision?
The decision may be correctly recorded and preserved in the minute book, but most corporations are not happy for just anyone to look through the records, anymore than you would want just anyone to look through your diary. When necessary, however, it is possible to take a bit of the minute book out and certify the excerpt as being accurate and a genuine record of the corporation's decision. The need for this will affect the way minutes of meetings and, particularly, resolutions are written. The person usually responsible for excerpting and certifying the records is the corporate secretary who is also responsible for seeing that the minutes of meetings are in good order.

On the following page is a certified copy of the resolutions adopted in the example of a directors' consent without formal meeting on page 22. Notice the secretary has drafted the resolution so that, when they are excerpted, it makes sense. That is, you can read just the resolution out of the context of the rest of the minutes and tell what decision is being made, what authority is being granted and to whom. Suppose the seller of the vacant lot next door to the company office wants to make sure that the company president really has authority to negotiate the purchase of the property. By looking at the following certificate, the seller, without being shown the full record of the board's deliberations on the matter, will be able to see that the president does have the necessary authority.

Notice that the secretary has represented that she is indeed the secretary and she would also place the corporation's official seal next to her signature. The presence of the seal is important. It means that anyone reading the document is able to rely on the truth of it without double checking to make sure that the person signing really is the secretary and is representing the corporation in this matter. Form 13 is for your corporate secretary to use to certify resolutions of the directors and Form 14 to certify resolutions of shareholders. Below is an example of such a certification in which the resolution has been copied from the minutes of the meeting. If a separate resolution sheet (Form 11 or Form 12) had been used, a copy of the resolution sheet could simply be attached.

Resolution certified by the corporate secretary—

Certified Copy of Resolutions Adopted by
the Board of Directors of

_____ Scrupulous Corporation _____

I HEREBY CERTIFY that I am the Corporate Secretary of _____ _____ Scrupulous Corporation _____, that the following is an accurate copy of res- olution(s) adopted by the Board of Directors of ___ Scrupulous Corporation ___ _____, effective _____ July 10 _____, _1997_, and that such resolutions continue in effect as of the date of this certification:

RESOLVED, that the President is authorized and directed to negotiate a contract for the purchase of the lot adjacent to the company's headquarters as described in his report (management storage file No. 94-56) for a cash purchase price of not more than $145,000.

FURTHER RESOLVED, that the officers of the corporation are authorized to execute such contract together with such other doc- uments as may be necessary or desirable to complete the described purchase within 120 days of the date of this resolution.

Signed and the seal of the Corporation affixed, _____ July 21 _____, _1997_ .

Roberta Moore
_____
Roberta Moore
Secretary

BOARD OF DIRECTORS 2

THE PLACE OF THE DIRECTORS IN THE CORPORATION

The Model Business Corporation Act (or "MBCA") says "all corporate powers shall be exercised by or under the authority of, and the business and affairs of the corporation managed under the direction of, its board of directors..." (Sec. 8.01). It is tempting to invent analogies to explain the relative roles of shareholders, directors and officers in a corporation. None of them are very useful and all are misleading in some way. Are the directors the brains and the executives the body of a corporation? (The word comes from *corporare*, i.e., to make into a body.) There's some truth to that, but you do want your executives to have brains of their own, don't you?

It's important to know what directors are not. A director ordinarily does not "represent" the corporation. Just because you are a director does not mean you have any power to act as agent for the corporation by negotiating deals or signing contracts or for any other purpose. A single director has no power and can not act alone (unless of course he or she is the *sole* director). Only the *board* of directors (or a committee of the board) can make a decision, and that must be done in a meeting or by written consent as described in chapter 1.

THE SIZE OF THE BOARD OF DIRECTORS

There's no one right size for a board of directors. What works for one may not for another, and what works at one stage of a corporation's development may not work later. It depends a lot on the personalities of the people involved. Do you work well with a group? Are there people (usually shareholders) who will feel left out or be disgruntled if they are not made directors? Maybe someone genuinely deserves a voice on the board. Maybe such people will be less trouble on the board than off. In one case a group of shareholders constantly complained that the board of directors was not declaring dividends frequently enough or big enough. After years of complaining, they finally gained representation on the board, and, faced with the true responsibility of running the company, immediately voted to cut the dividends further.

The articles of incorporation creating your corporation probably refers to an initial board of directors, specifying the number of members, and may or may not list the names of its members. The initial board, if it is named in the articles, will constitute the board until a change is made. (It's possible that the articles will say that the board, meaning not just the initial board but the permanent board will have a specified number of members. If such is the case, only an amendment to the articles of incorporation can change the number. But that is rare. See chapter 10.)

Usually the bylaws will specify the size of the board, in which case the number may be changed by amendment to the bylaws; or the bylaws will specify a range within which the number may be set by simple resolution of the directors or shareholders.

CHANGING THE
SIZE OF THE
BOARD BY
RESOLUTION

Your bylaws may say something like "The number of directors constituting the board of directors shall be not fewer than three nor more than nine as may be fixed from time to time, within such range, by the shareholders or by the board of directors." If the bylaws specify a range for the size of the board, a resolution adopted by the board of directors or the shareholders (check your bylaws to see if it's one or the other or either) will set the board at the size you want. If you have a choice, it may be better to have this resolution adopted by the board rather than the shareholders. Once the shareholders adopt a resolution, there may be some doubt as to whether the board can then adopt a subsequent resolution changing what the shareholders have done. Thus, once the shareholders have acted, the board may then be limited. Resolutions may be adopted either at a meeting (and incorporated into the minutes of the meeting using Form 1, 2, 5 or 6) or by written consent (by incorporating it into Form 4 or Form 8), or by separate resolution documents (Form 9 or Form 10). The following is an example of a resolution to change the size of the board of directors.

R-1.   Resolution increasing (or decreasing) the size of the board of directors—

Pursuant to **[Article/Section/Paragraph No.]** of the bylaws of the corporation, it is hereby RESOLVED, that effective **[Date]**, the number of directors constituting the board of directors shall be **[Number]**, and that such shall be the number of members of the board of directors until changed in a manner authorized by the articles of incorporation and the bylaws of the corporation.

CHANGING THE
SIZE OF THE
BOARD BY
AMENDMENT TO
THE BYLAWS

Your bylaws may say something like "the number of directors constituting the board of directors shall be three" making no reference to a range of numbers. If so, you may change the number by amending the bylaws. Check the section of your bylaws which tells how the bylaws may be amended. It probably will say that the amendment may be accomplished by a vote of the directors, but it may require a vote of the shareholders for some purposes. The following is an example of a resolution to change the bylaws, which would be used in Form 9 or Form 10, depending upon your corporation's rules for how bylaws must be changed.

> ### R-2. Resolution increasing (or decreasing) the size of the board by amendment to the bylaws—
>
> RESOLVED, that the first sentence of **[Article/Section/Paragraph No.]** of the bylaws of the corporation is hereby amended to read as follows:
>
> "The number of directors constituting the board of directors shall be **[Number]**."

ELECTING DIRECTORS

Directors are elected by the shareholders. Ordinarily the election takes place at the annual shareholders meeting (see chapter 5 for discussion of the relevant forms), In most corporations, the vote required is a majority of those present and voting at the meeting. On some occasions directors may be elected at a special meeting (using Form 6), or without there being a meeting at all (using Form 8). Remember that anything that can be done in a shareholders' meeting may be done by written consent if it is signed by all of the shareholders. Of course, that means you have to have unanimous approval for the election rather than just the majority's vote. The following is an example of the resolution to elect directors, which would be used in Form 5, 6, or 8, depending upon when, and whether, a meeting is held.

> ### R-3. Shareholders' resolution electing directors—
>
> RESOLVED, that the following individuals are hereby elected as directors of the corporation to serve until their successors are qualified and elected:
>
> ### [Insert list of names]

Of course, you cannot require a person to serve as director without his or her consent. In most cases, a chosen director's written consent is not necessary, but it doesn't hurt. There are a few situations, for example, if the corporation is subject to Securities and Exchange Commission proxy rules (see chapter 5) where written consent is required. Written consent does not prevent the director from resigning any time. The following statement (Form 15), alone or incorporated into a letter from the nominee director to the corporation will suffice:

Director's consent to serve—

Date: July 10, 1995
To: The Board of Directors, Scrupulous Corporation

    I hereby consent to serve as director of Scrupulous Corporation if elected.

Henry Hardy
Henry Hardy

Ordinarily, directors who are not also officers of the corporation (and therefore paid an officer's salary for the services they provide) receive some type of remuneration. The payments can be calculated in any number of ways, but most often consist of a daily allowance (or per diem) plus some form of reimbursement for travel, lodging and the like. Usually the directors themselves set the remuneration, sometimes at the recommendation of management.

A simple resolution preserved in the minutes of the directors meetings will suffice, although, the bylaws could also be drafted to provide for compensation. On the following page is an example of a directors resolution that provides different levels of compensation for directors who must travel substantial distances and those who live close to the site of the meeting. Such a resolution would be incorporated into either Form 1, 2, or 4.

R-4. Directors' resolution establishing directors' fees—

WHEREAS, management of the corporation has recommended to the board of directors a system for the remuneration of directors for their services, and

WHEREAS, the board, after consideration, has concluded that the recommendations of management are in the best interests of the corporation in maintaining a board of directors the members of which are able and willing to serve, it is therefore,

RESOLVED, that each director of the corporation shall be paid the following fees:

1. For attendance at each meeting or series of meetings lasting fewer than three hours — $[amount].
2. For attendance at each meeting or series of meetings lasting three hours or more in one day — $[amount].
3. For each overnight stay away from the director's usual residence required by attendance at a meeting or series of meetings, in addition to the fees provided above — $[amount] plus reimbursement for lodgings up to $[amount] per night.
4. For travel involving distances more than [number of miles] miles to or from a meeting, directors shall be reimbursed for the actual cost of such travel. Travel by private automobile shall be reimbursed at the rate and in the manner provided for reimbursement of employees of the company from time to time.

RESIGNATION, REMOVAL, AND REPLACEMENT OF DIRECTOR

Directors are usually elected for terms of one year each. It sometimes happens, however, that vacancies may occur on the board of directors at other times. Directors may resign whenever they wish, or they may die. And it may be that a director is removed by the shareholders for one reason or another.

REMOVAL OF A
DIRECTOR BY
THE
SHAREHOLDERS

Most states allow the shareholders of a corporation to vote for the removal of a director from office before his or her term is over. It may be done either in a meeting or by unanimous written consent. In some corporations, the articles of incorporation allow removal of a director only *for cause*.

In some corporations, directors are elected by groups of voters. For example, the holders of preferred shares may elect one director, and the holders of common shares may elect two. If this is the case, only the group of shareholders who elected the director may remove him or her. Another complication may arise if the shareholders elected the directors *cumulatively* (see chapter 5). In that case, a director may not be removed if the number of votes against the removal would be enough to elect the director by cumulative voting. In either case, a careful review of your state's law and your articles of incorporation is in order. Professional legal advice is always desirable.

If the removal takes place at a meeting, as opposed to by unanimous written consent, the notice of the meeting (Form 29 or Form 30) should inform the shareholders that one of the purposes of the meeting is to remove a director and to fill the vacancy created by such removal. On the following page is an example of a resolution suitable for adoption by the shareholders in a meeting (using Form 5 or Form 6) or by unanimous written consent (using Form 8). The resolution provides for removal for cause of a director who has been consistently absent from board meetings.

Where it is not required to state a cause, it is usually best not to state one in the formal resolution, and in that case, the first two paragraphs of the following example should be omitted. Of course, in the shareholders meeting, there may be discussion of the reasons for asking the shareholders to remove the director (be careful to avoid defamatory statements!), and that discussion may be recorded in the minutes of the meeting without being part of the resolution.

> ## R-5. Resolution for removal of a director by the shareholders—
>
> WHEREAS, it has been reported by the secretary of the corporation that **[name of director being removed]**, a director of the corporation, has **[describe the director's conduct or the situation justifying removal]**, and
> WHEREAS, it has been recommended to the shareholders that, for the reason stated above, **[name of director being removed]** should be removed from the board of directors, it is therefore
> RESOLVED, that effective on the day this resolution is finally adopted, **[name of director being removed]** shall be removed from the board of directors of the corporation, thereby creating a vacancy.

RESIGNATION OF A DIRECTOR

When a director resigns, it is usually done by a written notice directed to the corporation, its president or its board of directors. It could be done without a writing, but there is less chance of confusion if there is a signed piece of paper somewhere that definitely states the director's intent and the effective date of the resignation. There is no need to give a reason for the resignation, but often a resigning director will. If the corporation is publicly held (see chapter 5), the Securities and Exchange Commission has special rules about making public the reasons for a director's resignation.

Resignation of a director—

> Date: July 15, 1995.
> To: The Board of Directors of Scrupulous Corp.
>
> I hereby resign as director of Scrupulous Corp. effective July 31, 1995, at 5:00 p.m., EDT.
>
> Sincerely,
>
> *Evan Ewing*
>
> Evan Ewing

Once a vacancy has occurred on the board of directors, it may be filled either by the shareholders or by the remaining directors. An example of a resolution for the replacement of a director by the shareholders following the director's voluntary retirement is found after the heading "Consent to action without a meeting by shareholders—" on page 22.

The following are two examples of a resolution to replace a director, one by the shareholders and the other by the remaining directors. This type of resolution would be included in Form 1, 2, 4, 5, 6, or 8, depending upon whether it is adopted in a meeting or by written consent.

R-6.   Replacement of a director by the shareholders—

WHEREAS, the [death/resignation/removal] of [name of old director] as a director of the corporation has created a vacancy on the board of directors, and

WHEREAS, the shareholders wish to fill the vacancy promptly, it is therefore

RESOLVED, that [name of new director] is hereby elected to serve as director of the corporation for the remainder of the term for which [name of old director] was elected and until his successor is qualified and elected.

R-7.   Replacement of a director by the remaining directors—

WHEREAS, the [death/resignation/removal] of [name of old director] as a director of the corporation has created a vacancy on the board of directors, and

WHEREAS, the remaining directors, pursuant to [Article/Section/Paragraph] of the bylaws of the corporation wish to fill the vacancy promptly, it is therefore

RESOLVED, that [name of new director] is hereby elected to serve as director of the corporation for the remainder of the term for which [name of old director] was elected and until his successor is qualified and elected.

It frequently happens that the secretary of the corporation will be asked to assure someone dealing with the corporation that certain individuals are in fact the directors of the corporation. Form 16 will serve the purpose, and the following is an example.

Secretary's certification of board membership—

Certification of Secretary of Board of Directors Membership of

Scrupulous Corporation

I HEREBY CERTIFY that I am the Corporate Secretary of _____
_____Scrupulous Corporation_____, that the individuals listed below are the duly elected directors of the Corporation, and that they continue to hold the office of director on the date of this certification:

Raymond Rodriguez   Henry Hardy
Della Driskell   Calvin Collier

Signed and the seal of the Corporation affixed, __July 15, 1997_____.

Roberta Moore
Roberta Moore
Secretary

COMMITTEES OF THE BOARD OF DIRECTORS

Committees of the board of directors can be highly useful for some corporations. For one thing they streamline decision making by reducing the number of decision makers—it's easier to reach consensus among three committee members than, say, twelve board members. For another, it allows quicker reaction time. If your directors are scattered across the country, all with busy schedules, it is no easy chore to get them together for a meeting. But create a committee of directors who live close at hand, and you may be able to call a meeting on a few hours' notice. Finally, you can use a committee to concentrate the various areas of expertise of your board members on the matters most suited to their talents, for example, by creating an audit committee made up of board members with financial and accounting experience.

Committees may act within the powers granted to them by the bylaws or by the board. State laws do put some limitations on committee powers. Among other powers denied to committees, the Model Business Corporation Act includes the power to declare dividends, the power to adopt, amend or repeal bylaws, and the power to fill vacancies on the board or its committees (MBCA, Sec. 8.25).

CREATING A
COMMITTEE OF
THE BOARD

Committees may be created by the bylaws. Frequently, the bylaws will already provide for the existence of particular committees, and for these committees the board need only adopt a resolution appointing its members. (You must select the members from among the properly elected directors.) In most cases the bylaws will provide a mechanism for creating committees and appointing their members (usually by vote of a majority of the directors in office when the action is taken). Following are examples of two resolutions. The first creates a three member executive committee and appoints its members. The second increases the size of the committee and fills the vacancies created.

R-8. Directors' resolution creating a committee of the board—

RESOLVED, that there is hereby created an executive committee of the board of directors consisting of **[number of members]** members,

FURTHER RESOLVED, that to the extent permitted by law and the bylaws of the corporation, the executive committee shall have the full powers and act with the full authority of the board of directors when the board of directors is not in session, and

FURTHER RESOLVED, that the following individuals are hereby appointed to serve as members of the executive committee of the board of directors:

[insert list of members]

R-9.   Directors' resolution changing the size and membership of a committee—

RESOLVED, that the number of members of the executive commit-tee of the board of directors is hereby increased from **[current num-ber of committee members]** to **[new number of members]**, and

FURTHER RESOLVED, that the following individuals are hereby appointed to fill the vacancies created by the foregoing increase in the size of the executive committed and to serve as members of such committee.

[insert list of members]

KINDS OF
COMMITTEES

There can be many kinds of committees. A corporation is free to pick and choose among them or to create new committees for any purpose that seems useful, consistent with limitations imposed by law. There can be standing committees with regularly scheduled meetings, and there can be special *ad hoc* committees created to fill a temporary need. The latter are particularly useful when some issue raises a conflict of inter-est with one or more members of the board. An *ad hoc* committee may be created which excludes the conflicted directors and allows the remaining impartial directors to form a quorum and dispose of the issue with out their participation.

On the following two pages are four examples of resolutions amending the bylaws to create committees. These are four different kinds of com-mittees which are frequently found useful.

R-10. Amendment to the bylaws establishing an executive committee—

RESOLVED, that the bylaws of the corporation are hereby amended by the addition of a new **[Article/Section/Paragraph No.]** reading in its entirety as follows:

"There shall be an Executive Committee of the Board of Directors which shall, to the extent permitted by law, and subject to such limitations as may be imposed from time to time by such Board, exercise the powers of the Board of Directors when the Board is not in session. The number of members of the Executive Committee shall be established, and may be changed from time to time, by resolution of the Board of Directors. The members of the Executive Committee shall be appointed by a majority of the number of directors in office when the appointment is made and shall serve at the pleasure of such majority."

R-11. Amendment to the bylaws establishing an audit committee—

RESOLVED, that the bylaws of the corporation are hereby amended by the addition of a new **[Article/Section/Paragraph No.]** reading in its entirety as follows:

"There shall be an Audit Committee of the Board of Directors which shall supervise the auditing and examination of the books of account of the corporation by employees and independent auditors of the corporation. The Audit Committee shall meet with such independent auditors not fewer than **[number]** times during each fiscal year and shall have such other powers and duties as may from time to time be authorized by the Board of Directors. The number of members of the Audit Committee shall be established, and may be changed from time to time, by resolution of the Board of Directors. The members of the Audit Committee shall be appointed by a majority of the number of directors in office when the appointment is made and shall serve at the pleasure of such majority."

R-12. Amendment to the bylaws establishing a personnel committee—

RESOLVED, that the bylaws of the corporation are hereby amended by the addition of a new **[Article/Section/Paragraph No.]** reading in its entirety as follows:

"There shall be a Personnel Committee of the Board of Directors which shall consider and make recommendations to the Board of Directors regarding recruiting and compensating officers and senior employees of the corporation, the compensation of directors, compliance with applicable laws regarding employment practices, and other matters regarding personnel management, and shall have such other powers and duties as may from time to time be authorized by the Board of Directors. The number of members of the Personnel Committee shall be established, and may be changed from time to time, by resolution of the Board of Directors. The members of the Personnel Committee shall be appointed by a majority of the number of directors in office when the appointment is made and shall serve at the pleasure of such majority."

R-13. Amendment to the bylaws establishing a nominating committee—

RESOLVED, that the bylaws of the corporation are hereby amended by the addition of a new **[Article/Section/Paragraph No.]** reading in its entirety as follows:

"There shall be a Nominating Committee of the Board of Directors which shall consider available candidates for director of the corporation and shall make recommendations to the Board of Directors regarding the filling of vacancies which may occur from time to time in the membership of the Board of Directors. The number of members of the Nominating Committee shall be established, and may be changed from time to time, by resolution of the Board of Directors. The members of the Nominating Committee shall be appointed by a majority of the number of directors in office when the appointment is made and shall serve at the pleasure of such majority."

DIRECTORS MEETINGS 3

ACTION
WITHOUT
MEETINGS

Don't forget that any action that can be taken by the directors in a meeting can be taken without a meeting by written consent. (See chapter 1.)

HOW OFTEN
MUST WE HAVE
MEETINGS?

The bylaws of most corporations require only one "regular" meeting and that one follows the annual meeting of the shareholders. Many corporations have other regularly scheduled meetings. There is no rule on this. You have directors' meetings as often as it is useful. Many corporations find it useful to have regularly scheduled meetings, usually at least quarterly, timed to coincide with the availability of quarterly financial results. Some companies have them monthly or even weekly. It may depend on the condition of the company. A company going through difficult times may decide to have weekly meetings for a time until conditions improve.

One of the advantages of regularly scheduled meetings is that they are dependable. Your directors can plan schedules around regular meetings. Even if you cancel some of them due to a lack of anything to talk about, regular meetings save time and telephone calls, because you don't have to continually find dates when no one on the board has a scheduling conflict. Some corporations—especially small ones whose directors may also be day to day managers—don't have regularly scheduled meetings (other than the one following the annual shareholders meeting). These companies call "special" meetings whenever it is useful. Of course, even the corporations with frequent regular meetings may find it useful from time to time to call a special meeting.

If you have directors who are not involved in the company's affairs on a daily basis, you may owe it to them and to the corporation to have directors meetings frequently. If you don't, you may not allow the directors a fair chance to fulfill their duties to be informed and to make decisions in the best interests of the company and its shareholders.

WHO SHOULD
ATTEND
MEETINGS?

There's no rule on who should attend a directors meeting. Of course the directors must have notice of the meetings, and the board cannot conduct business without the necessary quorum. Common sense says that some representative of management should be present so that the directors will know what needs to be discussed and will be able to inquire about the company's condition. And there should be someone to record the minutes, usually the corporate secretary.

Beyond that, it's up to the directors. They need the people who can give them the information they need to make the decisions they have to make. It may include various officers and a wide variety of outside advisors such as lawyers, accountants, personnel experts, etc.

WHO MAY
ATTEND
MEETINGS?

Is there anyone who has a right to attend directors meetings other than the directors? Generally speaking, no. Some courts have said that a director has a right to insist on the presence of his or her own legal counsel for the purpose of giving advice about the director's duties or liabilities. Shareholders do not have a right to be informed about or to attend directors meetings without an invitation from the board. Neither do officers of the company who are not also members of the board.

NOTICE OF
DIRECTORS
MEETINGS

It is an important point of corporate law that you cannot have a meeting of the directors where business is conducted (i.e., where resolutions are adopted) unless notice goes to all the directors. Each director must have a fair chance to come to the meeting and to deliberate and vote. In the case of regularly scheduled meetings, notice is not necessary in most corporations, because regularity is notice enough. However, some companies' bylaws or articles of incorporation require notice even for regular meetings. Even is there is no requirement, it may be good practice or merely thoughtful to give the directors a reminder, especially if the regular meetings are infrequent. Form 17 is useful for that purpose.

For special meetings of the directors, notice is always necessary, and timing is important. The bylaws will say how far in advance of the meeting you have to give notice. Use Form 18.

FORMAT   There is no special format required for such notices, as long as the necessary information is included. For most companies, there is no requirement that notice be in writing. However, as is very frequently the case, writing is better because the writing will be around to provide proof that notice was given. Form 17 is a notice for a regular meeting, and Form 18 is for a special meeting. A notice can also be a simple letter on the corporate letterhead, as in the first of the two examples below.

Most bylaws do not require the notice to contain information about the matters to be discussed or decided at the meeting; although, many corporate managers make it a practice to enclose a proposed agenda, such as Form 20. Directors usually appreciate the information and it may allow the directors to be better prepared. Sooner or later, conscientious directors will insist on seeing reports and other information on which they are expected to rely *before* the meeting.

Notice of a regular meeting of directors—

Scrupulous Corporation
400 West 61st Avenue
P.O. Box 19
New York, NY 10032

October 3, 1997

Calvin Collier
123 Megabucks Avenue
New York, NY 10031

    RE: Notice of Meeting of Board of Directors

Dear Calvin

    This letter will remind you that the regular meeting of the ____Scrupulous____ ____Corporation____ board of directors will be held on _____November 6_____, __1997__. at __7:00__ p_m., at __the corporation conference room__ _____.

We hope you will be able to attend and that you will join us for lunch in the company dining room following the meeting.

    For your information, I have enclosed a tentative agenda together with several reports we will be discussing at the meeting.

                         Roberta Moore
                       _____
                       Roberta Moore
                       Corporate Secretary

Notice of a special meeting of directors—

NOTICE OF SPECIAL MEETING OF THE BOARD OF DIRECTORS OF

Scrupulous Corporation
_____

Date: October 3, 1997

TO: All Directors

There will be a special meeting of the board of directors on ___November 6___, ___1997___, at ___7:00___ ___p___.m., at ___the corporation conference room___
_____.

The primary purpose of this meeting is: Purchase of new truck.

Roberta Moore
_____
Roberta Moore
Corporate Secretary

Inevitably an occasion will arise when the required notice of a meeting doesn't get out, or doesn't get out in time, or there just isn't time to do it, or you forget. Fortunately the directors can waive notice *either before or after the meeting takes place and even if the director fails to show up for the meeting.* The waiver must be in writing. Of course you cannot require the director to waive notice, but if he or she will agree to do so voluntarily, Form 19 will serve the purpose. An example of such a waiver follows on the next page. Some corporations ask directors to sign such a form at each meeting just to take care of the possibility that, unknown to the corporate secretary, there has been a mistake in giving notice to which someone may later object. The Model Business Corporation Act says notice is automatically waived if the director shows up and participates in the meeting anyway (MBCA, Sec. 8.23).

Waiver of notice by a director—

Waiver of Notice of Meeting of Board of Directors of

Scrupulous Corporation

The undersigned director(s) of the Corporation hereby waive any and all notice required by law of by the articles of incorporation or bylaws of the Corporation, and consent to the holding of a ☒ Regular ❑ Special meeting of the Board of Directors of the Corporation on ___November 6, 1997___, at ___7:00___ _p_.m., at ___the corporation conference room___

Name: ___Henry Hardy___ Date: ___11/6/97___
Name: ___Robert Moore___ Date: ___11/6/97___
Name: ___Hugh Hardy___ Date: ___11/6/97___
Name: ___Raymond Rodriguez___ Date: ___11/6/97___
Name: ___Calvin Collier___ Date: ___11/6/97___
Name: ___Della Driskell___ Date: ___11/6/97___

What goes on at directors meetings varies from company to company and from time to time. Some are very formal and some very informal. It depends on the personalities of the people involved, the number of participants, and even the nature or number of issues to be discussed. There's no requirement that you have a formal agenda for a directors meeting, but it's usually worth the effort to make sure everything is covered. And directors like it. The following is an example of an agenda:

Sample agenda of a directors meeting—

AGENDA OF MEETING OF THE BOARD OF DIRECTORS OF

Scrupulous Corporation

Date of Meeting: November 6, 1997

1. Introductory remarks by the Chairman.
2. Approval of the minutes of last meeting.
3. Report of the Chief Financial Officer.
4. Salary report of V.P.-Personnel.
5. Other business.
6. Adjournment.

(Lunch to be served approximately 12:15 p.m. in the company dining room.)

KEEPING
RECORDS
For a discussion of the importance of the corporate minute book and keeping good records, refer to chapter 1.

It's the duty of the corporate secretary to see that accurate minutes are kept of all formal directors, shareholders or committee meetings, but that doesn't mean the secretary must be the one with a pencil and pad of paper at the meeting taking notes. Minutes may be recorded by anyone the secretary designates. It may be one of the company stenographers or one of the company's lawyers. When the board is in "executive session" (meaning that only directors and specifically designated persons are present), the minutes may be kept by one of the directors. Most people find it difficult to keep accurate minutes and participate in the meeting, so it is usually better to pick someone who is not expected to contribute to the discussion and can, therefore, concentrate on taking good notes.

The following are examples of minutes of a directors meeting, showing how various matters would be filled in for the description of events.

Minutes describing a report by an officer—

```
    The chairman of the meeting next asked Mr. Simpson, Vice President -
Operations, to present a report on efforts to upgrade the company's data pro-
cessing equipment.

    Mr. Simpson referred to a written report which had been distributed to
the directors in the information package accompanying the written notice of
the meeting (a copy of which may be found in management storage file No. 94-
58). He described in general terms the specifications of the system he
expects to recommend to the directors, and summarized the savings which may
be expected from personnel efficiencies to be gained through use of the pro-
posed system. He reported that he is continuing discussions with several
potential suppliers of equipment and expects to have firm bids from at least
three suppliers available for consideration by the Board at its next regu-
lar meeting.

    After brief questioning by several members of the Board, the Chairman
thanked Mr. Simpson for his thorough report and excused him from the meet-
ing.
```

Minutes describing a report by an independent auditor—

Mr. Tex A. Voydence, representing Bean-Counter Associates, the Company's independent auditors, and Mr. Calvin Collier, Treasurer, then joined the meeting. Mr. Voydence presented the completed audited financial statements of the Corporation for the fiscal year ended June 30, 1997, and a written report on the auditors' findings with regard to the Company's accounting and internal auditing procedures. A copy of the financial statements and audit report are located in management confidential file no. 97-739.

Mr. Voydence summarized the report. **[Describe highlights of report as presented by auditor]**. Mr. Voydence then asked whether there were any questions regarding the financial statements or the report.

Mr. Ray Rodriguez asked Mr. Collier whether management had any comments or questions regarding the information that had been presented. **[Describe comments of CFO and any additional questions.]**

The Chair of the meeting then suggested that the meeting go into executive session so that the directors could ask any additional questions they might have. Those present for the executive session were the directors and Mr. Voydence.

Ms. Della Driskell then asked Mr. Voydence to comment on the degree of cooperation the auditors had received from management and employees during the audit process. Mr. Voydence assured the directors that the Company had been highly cooperative and mentioned that Mr. Collier had been particularly helpful during the process.

Mr. Hugh Hardy asked whether there was any information that management had been reluctant to reveal to the auditors or had requested the auditors not to reveal to the directors. Mr. Voydence assured the board that there had not.

Ms. Driskell asked whether there had been any disagreements between management and the auditors about accounting methods or decisions or the presentation of the financial statements. Again, Mr. Voydence said that there had not.

Mr. Rodriguez asked whether there was any additional information that the auditors thought should be disclosed to the board or concerns that should be discussed. Mr. Voydence replied that there was not.

The Chair expressed the board's gratitude to Bean-Counter Associates for their good work, and the executive session was ended.

Sample directors' resolution accepting the report of a committee of the board—

> The Chairman next requested Ms. Driskell, Chair of the Personnel Committee to present the report of the Committee.
>
> Ms. Driskell informed the meeting that the Personnel Committee had met earlier in the day to consider compensation packages for senior officers of the company for the coming year. She distributed a report entitled "Compensation Scheme—1997" a copy of which is stored in Confidential Management File no. 94-13. It was the recommendation of the Personnel Committee that the salaries detailed on such report should be established by the Board as salaries for the coming year for the President, Senior Vice Presidents, Vice Presidents and Corporate Secretary, and that the health plan and other employee benefits in effect for the current year be carried over for the coming year.
>
> After brief discussion by the Directors, Mr. Rodriguez moved the adoption of the following resolution. The motion was seconded by Mr. Hardy and adopted by the unanimous vote of the Directors.
>
> RESOLVED, that the report and recommendations of the Personnel Committee presented to the Board are hereby adopted, that the salaries of the President, Senior Vice Presidents, Vice Presidents and Corporate Secretary for the fiscal year beginning January 1, 1998, shall be established at the rates shown on the report entitled "Compensation Scheme—1998" (Confidential Management File no. 96-13), and that the employee health plan and other benefits as described in the "Scrupulous Corp. Employee Benefits Handbook, 1997" shall be continued during such fiscal year.
>
> The Chairman thanked Ms. Driskell and the other members of the Personnel Committee for its excellent work.

Frequently, the corporate secretary will be asked to certify the authenticity of various actions by the board of directors. Form 11 is a certification of minutes of a board of directors meeting. Following are two examples of such a certification, one for when the Secretary is asked to certify the minutes of an entire meeting (Form 11), and one for a particular resolution (Form 13).

Corporate secretary's certification of the minutes of a board meeting—

Certified Copy of Minutes of Meeting of
the Board of Directors of

<u>   Scrupulous Corporation   </u>

    I HEREBY CERTIFY that I am the Corporate Secretary of <u>   </u>

<u>   Scrupulous Corporation   </u>, and that the following is an accurate copy of minutes of the meeting of the Board of Directors of the corporation, held on <u> May 17 </u>, <u>1997</u> :

        See attached copy of minutes.

Signed and the seal of the Corporation affixed, <u> September 22 </u>, <u>1997</u> .

                         Roberta Moore

                         Roberta Moore
                         Secretary

Corporate secretary's certification of a particular resolution of the board—

Certified Copy of Resolutions Adopted by
the Board of Directors of

<u>   Scrupulous Corporation   </u>

    I HEREBY CERTIFY that I am the Corporate Secretary of <u>   </u>

<u>   Scrupulous Corporation   </u>, that the following is an accurate copy of resolution(s) adopted by the Board of Directors of the corporation, effective <u> May 17 </u>, <u>1997</u>, and that such resolutions continue in effect as of the date of this certification:

        See attached copy of resolution.

Signed and the seal of the Corporation affixed, <u> September 22 </u>, <u>1997</u> .

                         Roberta Moore

                         Roberta Moore
                         Secretary

SHAREHOLDERS 4

THE PLACE OF THE SHAREHOLDER IN THE CORPORATION

Shareholders are not the corporation, and they don't represent the corporation. Like an individual director, an individual shareholder has no power to bind the corporation or to make a decision for the corporation (unless, of course there is only one shareholder). The shareholders own the corporation, but they don't own the assets of the corporation and have no rights as such to use or exercise control over any asset of the corporation. Shareholders do have the power, acting as a body, to act as the ultimate decision makers for the corporation, deciding certain fundamental issues directly and the rest indirectly through the election of directors. This and the next chapter are mostly about how shareholders make those decisions.

CREATING SHAREHOLDERS

What does it mean to own a share? You become a shareholder by buying or otherwise acquiring ownership of a share of the stock (meaning the supply of capital) of the corporation. Shareholders have two important rights: First, the right to vote in shareholders meetings, thereby exercising control over the corporation. Second, the right to share in distributions of the corporation's profits and, in case the corporation dissolves, its assets.

What is par value? Really, par value is not anything. In the last century, when corporation law was relatively primitive, par value had a useful purpose in that it represented a sort of core value, the amount of capital the company needed to begin and maintain its business. That amount of capital (the "authorized capital" the corporation was allowed by its articles of incorporation to raise) divided by the number of shares that could be issued by the company equaled the par value of each share. If a corporation sold shares for less than par value, a prohibited practice, the shares were said to be "watered."

But there was no standard for determining what the authorized capital of any particular corporation should be, so incorporators would choose a convenient figure that yielded a par value comfortably less than the expected selling price of the shares. In many cases it was one dollar. Sometimes the authorized capital would be determined merely by the tax rates imposed by statute on new corporations. For example, the statute might charge a minimum tax of $40.00 on new corporation filings which would permit the creation of a company with up to $100,000 in authorized capital. As a result, most start up companies in that state would have $100,000 in authorized capital and be permitted to sell 100,000 shares of stock, par value $1.00 per share. This said nothing about how much capital the company could raise, since $1.00 par value shares could be sold for any amount above that price. So, if the corporation sold 50,000 shares for $200 each, it would collect $10 million in capital.

You can see that par value provides no useful information about the value of a company, and for that reason, modern corporation laws make par value optional. That is, they permit "no par" stock. Some states eliminate the concept entirely. Most corporations, however, do still have par value shares (if for no other reason than blindly following tradition).

What does a stock certificate do? A stock certificate is not a share of stock. It certifies that the person named on the certificate is the owner or *holder* of the number of shares stated on the certificate. As long as certain basic information is included on the certificate, any format will do, if it is adopted by the directors as the company's official certificate form. It can be a plain sheet of paper with the information typed on, or it can be an elaborately engraved form with nice pictures. Form 21 is a simple common stock certificate. [For more elaborate stock certificates (and details about corporate formation), Sourcebooks, Inc., offers four books: *How to Form Your Own Corporation* (applicable in all fifty states and the District of Columbia), *How to Form a Simple Corporation in Florida*, *How to Form a Simple Corporation in Minnesota*, and *How to Form a Simple Corporation in Texas*. These should be available from your local bookstore, or they may be ordered directly from the publisher from the information in the back of this book.]

The front side of Form 21 indicates ownership of shares. Usually certificates are numbered sequentially from the first certificate issued. The term "fully paid and non-assessable" means at least the par value of the shares (for example, $1.00 par value shares multiplied by 150 shares owned equals $150) has been collected by the corporation in payment for the shares and that the shareholder is, therefore, not subject to further assessment related to the shares, no matter how much money the corporation may lose or need. "Transferable only on the books of the corporation" means that a purchaser of the shares from the holder named on the certificate will not be recognized as the new owner until the change of ownership is recorded in the stock records of the company. That will be done only if the named holder or the holder's authorized agent (or "attorney"—it doesn't have to be a lawyer) appears in person to direct that the change in ownership be recorded.

This transfer procedure may be accomplished by use of the form which usually appears on the back of a stock certificate, which is actually a power of attorney. Frequently the name of the attorney-in-fact is left blank and later filled in with the name of the secretary or treasurer of the corporation who actually records the transfer on the company books. There is a blank space for the shareholder's social security number or taxpayer identification number. It's there to help the company with its IRS reporting obligations.

Stock certificates are usually signed by two officers of the company. Which two varies from company to company. Check your bylaws to see what is appropriate. The paragraph beginning "Upon request…" is used only where the corporation is authorized to issue more than one class or series of shares (which will be discussed later). Following is an example of a simple stock certificate.

Common stock certificate—

Front side:

Certificate No.:_____000004_____   No. of Shares:__20,000____

_____SCRUPULOUS CORPORATION_____

Incorporated under the laws of the State of __Nevada_____
Authorized Capital Stock:__100,000_____ shares.
Par Value: ❏ $_____ per Share   ☒ No Par Value

    THIS CERTIFIES THAT __Henry Hardy_____
is the owner of _____20,000_____ fully paid and nonassessable shares of the
capital stock of _____Scrupulous Corporation_____ transferable
only on the books of the corporation by the holder of this certificate in person or by the
holder's duly authorized attorney upon surrender of this certificate properly endorsed.

    Upon request, and without charge, the corporation will provide written information as to the designations, preferences, limitations, and relative rights of all classes and series of shares and the authority of the board of directors to determine the same for future classes and series.

    IN WITNESS WHEREOF, __Scrupulous Corporation_____
has caused this certificate to be signed by its duly authorized officers and its corporate
seal to be affixed on __January 8, 1996_____.

                          *Raymond Rodriguez*_____,
                          President

                          *Roberta Moore*_____, Secretary

Back side:

FOR VALUE RECEIVED, the undersigned hereby sells, assigns and transfers to
_____ , _____ of the shares
represented by the certificate on the reverse side, and irrevocably appoints
_____ attorney, with full power of
substitution, to transfer such shares on the books of <u>Scrupulous Corporation</u>.

DATED: _____ , _____ .

_____

Witness: _____

Social Security Account Number or other Taxpayer Identification Number of the
assignee: _____

BUYING AND SELLING SHARES OF STOCK

REGULATORY
ISSUES

The Securities and Exchange Commission and Blue Sky laws. Since the 1930's, the buying and selling of corporate securities (a term which includes stocks and bonds) has been carefully regulated by both the Federal and state governments. The Securities and Exchange Commission is the Federal agency with responsibility to administer U.S. laws on the subject, chiefly the Securities Act of 1933 and the Exchange Act of 1934. State statutes on the subject, called *Blue Sky* laws, are usually administered by the Secretary of State, the same official that oversees incorporations and other corporate matters.

The details of securities regulation are beyond the scope of this book. But you should know that the regulatory scheme says that *every* sale of a corporate security (whether the seller is the corporation or an individual investor) is regulated and can only take place if "registered" in the manner required by law unless a specific exemption from the requirement is available. Registration of securities is a costly and difficult process, so it's fortunate that exemptions are plentiful. However, there must be an exemption or there must be a registration. Even an inadvertent violation of these requirements can be even more costly.

How do you know if there is an exemption available to you? The sale of a small number of shares to a very few shareholders who will be closely involved in the operation of the company will almost certainly be exempt from registration. But the only certain answer to the question depends on the facts in each case. If there is any doubt, competent legal advice is essential.

ORIGINAL ISSUE SHARES

Original issue shares are those sold by the issuing corporation to the shareholders, as opposed to shares which, once issued, may be sold by the shareholder to another person. The sale of original issue shares is done pursuant to a contract between the company and the investor called a "stock subscription agreement." Form 22 is a stock subscription agreement, and the following is an example:

Stock subscription agreement—

Stock Subscription Agreement

SCRUPULOUS CORPORATION

In consideration of the mutual promises contained in this agreement and other lawful and sufficient consideration, the receipt of which is hereby acknowledged, _____
__Scrupulous Corporation__ (the "Corporation"), a ____Nevada____ corporation, agrees to issue, and the undersigned purchaser agrees to subscribe to and purchase __20,000__ shares of the ____common stock____ of the Corporation for cash at the price of $__10,000.00__ . The purchase price for the shares shall be payable in full upon issuance of the shares by the Corporation.

Purchaser: __Henry Hardy, 238 Prosperity Street, New York, NY 10032__

__Soc. Sec. No. 999-99-9999__

(Name, address, and social security number of taxpayer identification number of purchaser)

Henry Hardy
(Signature of Purchaser)

Corporation

By: *Roberta Moore*

STOCK OPTIONS   A *stock option* is the right to buy shares of stock in the future at a pre-determined price. Such arrangements are often used as employee incentives under the assumption that an employee who has the right to buy shares five years from today at today's prices will work extra hard to make sure that, in five years, the company's shares will be worth more than today. An investor who believes the value of the company will increase over time will see the purchase of an option as a valuable asset.

The sale or other transfer of an option to buy shares is also subject to the Securities and Exchange Commission and Blue Sky regulations. In addition to the possibly complex issues resulting from that regulation, the tax consequences of stock options and employee incentive plans need to be considered (these are beyond the scope of this book).

An option contract must, like any other contract, be supported by some bargained for consideration. If there is no consideration, then the promise of the corporation to sell its stock for the stated price is not enforceable in the courts. The option may be given as employee compensation; or the consideration could be any number of things such as money, or a promise to work for the company or to assume new duties.

Below is an example of a resolution to grant an option as employee compensation. Form 23 is an option agreement form, and on the following page is an example of such an agreement.

R-14.   Directors' resolution granting a stock option to an officer—

RESOLVED, that for value received, there is hereby granted to **[name and title of grantee]** (the "Grantee") an option to purchase **[number of shares subject to the option]** shares of the **[class and series of shares]** of the corporation. The purchase price of the shares will be $**[amount]** per share, payable in cash upon the exercise of the option. The option shall be evidenced by and subject to the terms and conditions of a written Stock Option Agreement in the form presented by management to and hereby approved by the directors on the date this resolution is adopted, and further

RESOLVED, that management of the corporation is hereby authorized and directed to take such action and execute such documents as may be necessary or desirable to give effect to the foregoing resolution.

Option to purchase shares—

Stock Option Agreement

Scrupulous Corporation

In consideration of the mutual promises contained in this agreement and other lawful consideration, the receipt and sufficiency of which is hereby acknowledged, Scrupulous Corporation (the "Corporation), a Nevada corporation, hereby grants to Della Driskell (the "Grantee") an option to purchase shares of the Corporation upon the following terms and conditions:

1. Consideration of the Grantee. The grant of an option in this agreement is made in consideration of providing marketing services to the corporation.

2. Number of shares and price. The option granted in this agreement (the "Option") is an option of the Grantee to purchase 2,000 shares of the common shares of the Corporation. The purchase price of the shares will be $2.00 per share, payable in cash upon the exercise of the option.

3. Time and method of exercise. The Option may be exercised in whole or in part by the Grantee at any time and from time to time before December 31, 1999 by delivery to the Corporation at its principal office written notice of the Grantee's intent to exercise the option stating the number of shares being purchased and accompanied by the purchase price of the shares being purchased. The option may be exercised as to whole numbers of shares only.

4. Adjustments of the number of shares subject to the Option. In the event of any share dividend, share split or other recapitalization affecting the shares of the Company, or a merger of the Corporation in which it is the surviving corporation, the number of shares subject to the Option will be automatically adjusted to equitably reflect such change or merger. In the event of the dissolution of the Corporation, or a merger or other fundamental change following which no shares of the corporation may be issued, the Option will terminate, but the Grantee will have a reasonable opportunity to exercise the Option immediately before such event. Except as provided in this paragraph, the Grantee shall have no rights as a shareholder of the Corporation with respect to the shares subject to the Option until such shares are issued upon exercise of the Option.

5. No transfer. The Option may not be transferred by the Grantee other than by will or the laws of inheritance.

The Corporation and the Grantee have executed this Stock Option Agreement under seal on August 22, 1997.

Grantee:

Della Driskell

Della Driskell

Corporation:

By: *Raymond Rodriguez*

Raymond Rodriguez,   President

Attest:

Roberta Moore

Roberta Moore,   Secretary

Once it has been agreed that original issue shares will be sold pursuant to a subscription agreement, option agreement, or other circumstances, it may be appropriate for the directors to authorize the actual issuance of shares to the purchasers. They may do so in a resolution such as the example below. This resolution would be included in Form 1, 2 or 4.

When the corporation was created, it may have adopted a "Section 1244 Plan" under federal tax laws. Shares issued under such a plan receive favorable tax treatment if they are later sold for a loss or become worthless. If such a plan is in effect (you can tell by looking in the corporate minutes), the resolution issuing the shares should mention it.

R-15. Directors' resolution issuing stock—

WHEREAS, **[if applicable, add: "pursuant to a Section 1244 Plan adopted by the corporation on _____, _____,"]** the person(s) named below have **[agreed to purchase/exercised options for]** the number of shares stated opposite his or her name for the consideration indicated pursuant to **[a subscription agreement/an option agreement]** dated **[date of the agreement]**, it is therefore

RESOLVED, that the proper officers of the corporation are hereby authorized and directed, upon receipt by the corporation of the stated consideration, to issue certificates representing the number of **[class and series]** shares of the corporation indicated to the persons named below:

Name of purchaser   No. of shares $/share

BUYING AND
SELLING SHARES
ALREADY
ISSUED

A share of stock, like any other piece of property, may be sold or given away by its owner. Usually the owner can transfer shares without any advance permission from the corporation or other shareholders. (In smaller corporations there is sometimes a *shareholders' agreement* which places limits on the rights of an owner to dispose of his or her shares. See below in this chapter.) It is even possible for the ownership of shares to change without the corporation knowing about it, but few shareholders would want such a thing to happen. If the company doesn't know you are a shareholder, it won't know to send you the dividend check. Obviously it is important for the corporation to know who its owners are or at least be able to communicate with them, so there must be some list of shareholders and some way of amending the list. (Often the shares of large corporations are held in *street name* by *nominees*, and the corporation doesn't know the identity of many of its shareholders. This is to facilitate the transfer of shares through brokerage accounts. There is a system by which such corporations can communicate with their real shareholders through the nominees.)

The back side of the stock certificate, Form 21, serves two purposes. It is written evidence that the owner has transferred his or her shares to a new owner, and it authorizes the responsible officer of the company to amend the list of shareholders to include the new owner. After the endorsement form is completed and signed, the stock certificate would be turned over to the new owner who would then present it to the appropriate officer, usually the treasurer or secretary, who would change the shareholder list and issue a new certificate to the new owner. The officer will write "CANCELED" on the face of the old certificate and keep it with the list of shareholders. Notice that Form 21 allows some, but not all, of the shares represented by a certificate to be transferred to the new owner. Suppose the seller's certificate represents 1,000 shares of Scrupulous Corporation and he only wants to sell 250 of them to the new owner. The Certificate would be completed and turned over to the treasurer as usual, but the treasurer would issue two new certificates. One representing 750 shares issued to the seller and another representing 250 shares to the buyer. The witness may be any adult who has no interest in the transaction.

The example on the following page is the back side of the stock certificate form completed.

Endorsement of a stock certificate—

FOR VALUE RECEIVED, the undersigned hereby sells, assigns and transfers to Bertram Buyer, two hundred fifty (250) of the shares represented by the certificate on the reverse side, and hereby irrevocably appoints Roberta Moore, Corporate Secretary, attorney with full power of substitution, to transfer such shares on the books of Scrupulous Corp.

DATED: ___August 10___, 19_97_.

Raymond Rodriguez
Raymond Rodriguez

Witness:

C. M. Sine
C. M. Sine

Social Security Account Number or other Taxpayer Identification Number of the assignee: _000-00-0000_.

Occasionally it is inconvenient to use the endorsement printed on the stock certificate. For example, it may be desirable to complete the transaction by mail, and therefore safer to send the unendorsed certificate in one package and the document authorizing the transfer in another. Form 24, a Stock Powers Separate from Certificate, is used for this purpose instead of the endorsement form printed on the back side of the certificate.

On the following page is an example of such a form. Again, the witness may be any adult who has no interest in the transaction.

Stock powers separate from certificate—

Stock Powers Separate from Certificate

In exchange for valuable consideration, the receipt and sufficiency of which is hereby acknowledged, the undersigned hereby sells, assigns and transfers to _____Hugh Hardy_____, _____5,000_____ shares of the stock of __Scrupulous Corporation_____ registered on the books of the Corporation in the name of the undersigned and represented by Certificate(s) number__000010_____.

The undersigned hereby irrevocably appoints _____ ___Roberta Moore_____, _____Corporate Secretary_____, attorney, with full power of substitution, to transfer such shares on the books of the Corporation.

Executed on ___March 31, 1997_____.

Henry Hardy
_____
Henry Hardy

Witness:

Calvin Collier
_____
Calvin Collier

Social Security Account Number of other Taxpayer Identification Number of the assignee:___000-00-0000_____

There are many reasons a corporation may want to buy its shares from shareholders. For example, if the corporation is small, there is probably no market for the shares outside the corporation. A shareholder who is dissatisfied with the way the corporation is being run, but is not in a position to force a change in direction, may have no way to disassociate himself other than to sell the shares back to the company. Or, the corporation may merely wishes to reduce the number of its shareholders.

Some shares and other corporate securities are said to be *redeemable* which means that the corporation has the power to force the shareholder to sell the shares to the corporation under certain conditions. There can also be a class of shares that allow the shareholder to force the corporation to buy his or her shares. These subjects are beyond the scope of this book; however, the resolution on the following page is useful for the more common situation where the corporation and the shareholder agree, for whatever reason, that it would be useful for the corporation to acquire the shareholder's interest in the company.

There are some limits on the power of the directors to authorize such a purchase. It is, after all, a distribution of the company's money (or other assets) to a shareholder and is subject to the same limitations as the dividend (see chapter 6). Moreover, it is an unequal distribution. That is, the shareholder who sells shares to the company is getting a distribution of assets the other shareholders are not getting. The directors may have personal liability if the purchase of the shareholder's interest is unfair to the other shareholders, or unfairly advantageous to one of the directors voting in favor of it, or otherwise harmful to the company.

The articles of incorporation of some corporations forbid the company to resell shares which have been purchased from shareholders. In such a case, the number of shares authorized by the articles must be reduced by the number of shares repurchased. For example, suppose the articles of incorporation authorize a company to issue 1000 shares, and 250 of them have been issued to Shareholder A. The corporation would then have left 750 "authorized but unissued shares" which it could sell to other people. Suppose the corporation later repurchases the 250 shares from Shareholder A. According to the Model Business Corporation Act (Sec. 6.31), the repurchased shares again become "authorized but unissued" and the corporation would have 1000 of them to sell. *If the articles forbid the resale of shares purchased from shareholders*, then the number of "authorized but unissued" shares must somehow be reduced back to 750. (Notice that it does not matter that you do not intend to resell the shares. The number authorized must be reduced regardless.) It must be done by an amendment to the articles of incorporation (see chapter 10). Unlike most such amendments, the MBCA allows this one to be done by the directors with no shareholder vote. The company must file the amendment with the Secretary of State (or other appropriate agency in your state) where the company is incorporated.

Below is a resolution of the board of directors authorizing the repurchase of a shareholder's shares. It presumes that the corporation's articles of incorporation forbids it to resell such shares and that the articles must therefore be amended to reduce the number of authorized shares.

R-16. **Directors' resolution authorizing purchase of a shareholders' stock—**

WHEREAS, **[name of shareholder]** has offered to sell to the corporation, and the corporation wishes to purchase **[number of shares]** of the common stock of the corporation previously issued to such shareholder, it is therefore

RESOLVED, that the corporation shall purchase **[number of shares]** shares of the common stock of the company from **[name of shareholder]** for $**[amount]** per share, such transaction to take place on or before **[date]**, and further

RESOLVED, that articles of incorporation of the corporation are hereby amended to reduce the number of authorized common shares by the number of shares so purchased, such amendment to be effective on the date such transaction is completed or within a reasonable time thereafter, and further

RESOLVED, that the officers of the corporation are authorized and directed to file articles of amendment with the Secretary of State of **[state of incorporation]** giving effect to such amendment in a timely manner, and further

RESOLVED, that the officers of the corporation are authorized and directed to take such acts as may be necessary or desirable to give effect to the foregoing.

Sometimes it becomes desirable to increase or decrease the total number of shares of stock. Typically, an increase may be needed to create more capital for the corporation to expand. Decreases were discussed above. If any change is to be made, it will usually be done by a stockholders resolution to amend the articles of incorporation. Below is a resolution to increase or decrease the number of shares of the corporation.

> **R-17.** **Stockholders resolution to change number of shares—**
>
> RESOLVED, that the authorized capital stock of the corporation be **[increased/decreased]** to $**[amount]**, consisting of **[number of shares]** shares, with **[no par value/a par value of $_____]** per share, and
>
> RESOLVED, that the corporation's Articles of Incorporation shall be amended to reflect this change.

Below is an example of the type of form which must be filed with the state if it is necessary to amend the articles of incorporation. (Your state may require the use of a standard fill-in-the-blank form supplied by the state agency.) If (as is more likely) the articles do not forbid such resales, the third paragraph in the resolution above, and the following form, may be omitted. If your state does not have its own form for amending articles of incorporation, you can use Form 51. This can also be modified to increase the number of shares.

Articles of amendment reducing the number of authorized shares—

> ## Articles of Amendment of
>
> Scrupulous Corporation
> _____
>
> The Articles of Incorporation of __Scrupulous Corporation__
> _____are hereby amended as follows:
>
> 1. The name of the corporation is Scrupulous Corporation.
> 2. The number of authorized common shares of the corporation is hereby reduced by 10,000.
> 3. After such reduction, the number of common shares authorized shall be 90,000.
> 4. This amendment was adopted on October 26, 1997, by the board of directors without shareholder action as permitted by statute.
>
> The date of these Articles of Amendment is___November 9___,__1997__.
>
> Scrupulous Corporation
>
> By:_*Raymond Rodriguez*_____
> Raymond Rodriguez, President

AGREEMENTS AMONG SHAREHOLDERS

With few exceptions, shareholders have no duty to look out for each other. Each shareholder is free to vote her shares for her own interests even though it may not be in the best interests of the other shareholders or even the corporation (there are some limits on the damage a controlling shareholder is allowed to do), and each shareholder is allowed to sell her shares for the best price available to whoever is willing to pay it. This system works well for the shareholders of a corporate giant, but may not be the best way to run a small corporation. If there are only a few shareholders, most or all of whom are closely involved in the business, the identity of the other shareholders and their plans for the corporation may be critically important.

For this reason, shareholders enter into a variety of agreements among themselves about the way the corporation is to be managed. They may agree on who the officers and directors will be, or whether the corporation will be allowed to consider merger with another, or even what kind of business the corporation will be allowed to transact. Form 26 is an agreement among the shareholders of a corporation that each of the shareholders will be assured representation on the board of directors and a job as an officer.

Form 26 provides that each officer will have the same salary. Of course any number of possible arrangements could be made, but note that if the salaries are in the same proportion as share ownership, the IRS may argue that they are not salaries at all but dividends and therefore not deductible to the corporation.

Note also that the only shareholders bound by the agreement are the ones who sign it. Any new shares issued by the corporation may not be subject to the agreement. On the following page is an example of such a shareholders' agreement:

Shareholders' agreement regarding directors and officers—

Shareholders' Agreement

This agreement is made by and among ___Scrupulous Corporation___ _____ (the "Corporation") and the undersigned shareholders of the corporation (the "Shareholders" collectively, or "Shareholder" individually) on ___August 9, 1997___.

In consideration of the premises and of the mutual promises and conditions contained in this agreement, the Corporation and the Shareholders agree for themselves, their successors and assigns, as follows:

1. The number of directors of the corporation shall be ___4___. So long as he or she shall own shares in the Corporation, each Shareholder shall have the right to serve as a director of the Corporation or to designate a person to serve as director. Any such person named must be reasonably capable of performing the duties of a director.

2. So long as he or she shall own shares in the Corporation, each shareholder shall have the right, but shall not be required, to serve as an officer of the Corporation. The compensation paid to each Shareholder during each calendar year for his or her services as an officer of the Corporation shall be equal to the compensation paid to each other Shareholder of the corporation for services as an officer. The titles and duties of each Shareholder so employed by the Corporation shall be as determined by the Board of Directors from time to time.

3. The Shareholders shall vote their shares in such a way as to give effect to the provisions of this agreement.

4. Every certificate representing shares owned by the parties to this agreement shall prominently bear the following legend: "The shares represented by this certificate are subject to the provisions of a Shareholders' Agreement dated ___August 9, 1997___, a copy of which is on file in, and may be examined at, the principal office of the Corporation."

IN WITNESS WHEREOF, the parties have executed this Agreement under seal on the date indicated above.

Scrupulous Corporation

By: _Raymond Rodriguez_____
    Raymond Rodriguez, President

Attest: _Roberta Moore_____
    Roberta Moore, Secretary

_Henry Hardy_____
Henry Hardy,   Shareholder

_Calvin Collier_____
Calvin Collier,   Shareholder

_Hugh Hardy_____
Hugh Hardy,   Shareholder

_Della Driskell_____
Della Driskell,   Shareholder

The most common type of shareholders' agreement is one that places restrictions on the transfer of shares. The owners of a small business usually think of themselves as partners, more or less, even if the business is a corporation. The success of the business may depend on the personalities involved and how well they get along. If one "partner" sells his interest, or leaves it in his will, to someone the others detest, catastrophe may result.

A shareholders' agreement can prevent that by keeping each shareholder from transferring shares to an outsider without first offering it to the other shareholders for the same price or a price determined by formula. The existing shareholders get a chance to look the potential new shareholder over, and if they don't like what they see, they can buy the shares themselves. You may well ask why the contract doesn't simply say no shareholder can sell his shares without the permission of the others. The reason is that the courts won't enforce such an agreement. It is a "restraint on alienation" which is frowned on everywhere in the law.

Because courts very carefully interpret agreements that make it difficult for shareholders to sell their shares, and because the methods for determining the price at which the shares can be purchased are often complex and should be carefully tailored to each company, shareholders' agreements of this type are too long and complex to fit comfortably in this book.

CREATING A NEW CLASS OF SHARES

CLASSES AND
SERIES OF
SHARES

What are "classes" and "series" of shares, and do we need them? A class or series of shares is a group of shares that have the same rights as the others in the same class or series. Usually the rights in question are the right to vote (in which case the group is called a *voting group*), the right to receive dividends and the right to divide the assets of the corporation in the event it is dissolved. It may also refer to the right of the corporation to redeem the shares, as discussed above.

Traditionally there have been two broad classes of shares—*common* and *preferred*. Sometimes these classes have been subdivided into various series designated by letters or numbers. Modern corporation statutes allow almost unlimited flexibility in the design of various classes and series, so long as somewhere, among all the shares taken as a whole, the shareholders have all the power to vote on the issues that shareholders may vote on and have the right to receive all the remaining assets of the corporation upon dissolution.

Most corporations get along nicely without having more than one class of shares, and that class will be called the common shares. Common shares traditionally have one vote per share on all matters that may be voted on by shareholders and a right to receive dividends only if the directors decide to declare one. Preferred shares frequently have no voting rights except as granted by statute, but usually enjoy a predetermined dividend that the directors must declare and pay before they may pay a dividend on the common shares. Preferred shareholders may also enjoy a *preference* in dividing the corporate assets upon dissolution.

Preferred shares allow the corporation to sell shares for additional capital without unduly reducing the control powers enjoyed by the common shareholders. The preferred investors are willing to trade away the right to vote on mundane corporate matters such as the election of directors for the relative certainty of the preferred dividend.

CONVERTIBLE
SHARES

Convertible shares are those that, under certain circumstances, may be converted from one class or series into another, or even into another type of security such as from stock to bonds.

CREATING A
SEPARATE CLASS OF
SHARES IN THE
ARTICLES OF
INCORPORATION

The articles of incorporation describe the capital structure of the company. If there is only one class of shares, the description may be very simple, such as: "The number of shares the corporation is authorized to issue is 100,000." The shares then issued will be referred to as the common shares of the corporation.

Additional classes of shares may be created when the articles of incorporation are first filed, in which case the relevant provision will look more like the following example. The articles may also be amended later through resolution and filing articles of amendment (see chapter 10). In the example below, each type of stock would be listed by class, series (if any), par value (if there is no par value, simply type in "No par"), and number of shares of each type.

R-18.   **Provision of articles of incorporation establishing a class of preferred shares—**

RESOLVED, that Article **[article number]** of the articles of incorporation of the company is hereby amended to read as follows:

"Article **[article number]**. The number of shares the corporation is authorized to issue is **[total number of shares]** which shall be divided into two classes as follows:

Class	Series	Par value	Number of shares
[Common/Preferred]	**[if any]**	**[No par/amount]**	**[number of shares]**

The preferences, limitations and relative rights of each class and series of preferred shares shall be as determined by the board of directors pursuant to **[your state's version of MBCA, Sec. 6.02]** before the issuance of any shares of that class and series.'

POWER OF
DIRECTORS TO
ESTABLISH
PREFERENCES

The provision of the articles of incorporation could state in detail the preferences, limitations and relative rights of each class. If you know what they are at the time the articles are drafted, there is no reason not to do so. However, the MBCA allows later consideration of such details when the time comes to issue the first preferred shares. The directors may then decide on the preferences, and file an amendment to the articles with the state, as shown in the following two examples. Unlike most other amendments to the articles of incorporation, this is one that may be adopted by the directors without a vote of the shareholders. These examples show a typical arrangement for preferred shares, but do not by any means exhaust the possibilities. Different classes of shares can be designed in ways limited only by imagination, and can serve a wide variety of corporate and financial purposes.

R-19.   Directors' resolution establishing preferred stock—

RESOLVED, that pursuant to Article [article number] of the articles of incorporation of the corporation there is hereby created a class of Preferred Shares, Series A, with the preferences, limitations and relative rights stated in the following amendment to the articles of incorporation, and further

RESOLVED, that Article [article number] of the articles of incorporation of the company is hereby amended to read as follows:

"Article [article number]. The number of shares the corporation is authorized to issue is [number of shares] which shall be divided into two classes as follows:

Class	Series	Par value	Number of shares
Common		[No par/value]	[number of shares]
Preferred	A	[No par/value]	[number of shares]

When and if legally declared by the board of directors, the record holder of each share of Preferred stock, Series A, shall be entitled to receive cash dividends at the annual rate of $[amount] per share payable in equal quarterly installments beginning on [date]. Cash dividends on Preferred shares shall be cumulative from the first dividend payment following the issuance of the share, and shall be declared and paid, or set apart for payment, before any cash dividends shall be paid on the Common stock."

Note: The form above will need to be added to or modified if more than two classes of stock are created, or if the preferences of a particular class are different than in the example.

Amendment to articles of incorporation establishing preferred stock—

Articles of Amendment of

Scrupulous Corporation

The Articles of Incorporation of Scrupulous Corporation

are hereby amended as follows:

1. The name of the corporation is Scrupulous Corporation .
2. The following amendment to Article 6 of the articles of incorporation of the corporation was adopted by the board of directors on [date]:

Article 6 . The number of shares the corporation is authorized to issue is 100,000 which shall be divided into two classes as follows:

Class	Series	Par value	Number of shares
Common		No par	50,000
Preferred	A	No par	50,000

When and if legally declared by the board of directors, the record holder of each share of Preferred stock, Series A , shall be entitled to receive cash dividends at the annual rate of $ 1.00 per share payable in equal quarterly installments beginning on July 1 , 19 97 . Cash dividends on Preferred shares shall be cumulative from the first dividend payment following the issuance of the share, and shall be declared and paid, or set apart for payment, before any cash dividends shall be paid on the Common stock.

The date of these Articles of Amendment is July 19, 1997 .

Scrupulous Corporation

By: *Raymond Rodriguez*
Raymond Rodriguez, President

PREFERRED
STOCK
CERTIFICATES

Each class and series of stock should have its own form of certificate that can be clearly distinguished from the others so that purchasers will know what they are buying.

Form 25 is a share certificate for preferred stock The following is an example of such a certificate for 100 shares of preferred stock, series A, for Scrupulous Corp. Compare it to Form 21 (for common stock). The back side of the certificate is similar to that of Form 21.

Preferred stock certificate—

Front side:

Certificate No.: 000001-PA

No. of Preferred Shares, Series A : 10,000

Scrupulous Corporation

PREFERRED STOCK, SERIES A

Incorporated under the laws of the State of Nevada

Authorized Preferred Stock, Series A : 100,000 shares, No Par Value.

THIS CERTIFIES THAT Della Driskell
is the owner of 10,000 shares fully paid and nonassessable shares of the
capital stock of Scrupulous Corporation
transferable only on the books of the corporation by the holder of this certificate in person or by the holder's duly authorized attorney upon surrender of this certificate properly endorsed.

Upon request, and without charge, the corporation will provide written information as to the designations, preferences, limitations, and relative rights of all classes and series of shares and the authority of the board of directors to determine the same for future classes and series

IN WITNESS WHEREOF, Scrupulous Corporation
has caused this certificate to be signed by its duly authorized officers and its corporate seal to be affixed on April 10, 1997 .

Raymond Rodriguez , President
Raymond Rodriguez

Roberta Moore , Secretary
Roberta Moore

CERTIFICATION OF SHARES BY SECRETARY

On occasion it may become necessary to verify the total number of shares to some third party (such as a government agency, potential lender or investor, etc. Form 52 can be used for this purpose. Below is an example of Form 52 completed.

Certification of Secretary of

Scrupulous Corporation

    I HEREBY CERTIFY that I am the Corporate Secretary of _____
Scrupulous Corporation _____, that I am the custodian of the stock records of said corporation, and that the total number of shares of the capital stock of the corporation issued and outstanding on _____ May 31 _____, 1997 _____, is
100,000 no par value common _____ shares.

Signed and the seal of the Corporation affixed, _____ May 31 _____, 1997 .

Roberta Moore

Roberta Moore
Secretary

LOST OR DESTROYED STOCK CERTIFICATES

    A stock certificate is not a share of stock. It is only the physical representation of a share. When a certificate gets lost or destroyed, it does not affect the ownership of the share represented. But losing a certificate can be a headache for the corporation and, therefore, for the shareholder. Suppose a "lost" certificate representing 1,000 shares falls into the hands of a dishonest person who then sells the shares to an innocent buyer. If the corporation issues a new certificate for 1,000 shares to the original owner who lost the certificate, and the buyer later shows up with the original certificate asking to be recognized as a legitimate shareholder, suddenly the corporation may have more shares outstanding than it thought.

To prevent or at least minimize the damage caused by such an embarrassment, corporations have procedures for dealing with lost or destroyed certificates. They are usually found in the bylaws and are derived from the Uniform Commercial Code, not the business corporation statute. Normally the bylaws will require the owner of a lost, stolen or destroyed certificate to make representations to the corporation along the lines of Form 27, agreeing to indemnify the corporation if the replacement of the certificate results in any loss to the corporation (e.g., if the corporation later has to buy its own shares on the open market to issue to the "good faith purchaser" that later shows up in the way described above. Sometimes corporations require the shareholder to purchase a security bond to protect the corporation against such losses. On the following page is an example of Form 27 completed:

Shareholder's affidavit and indemnity regarding lost or destroyed certificate—

Lost or Destroyed Stock Certificate Indemnity Agreement and Affidavit

The undersigned, being duly sworn, hereby affirms the following:

1. The undersigned is record holder of _____500_____ shares (the "Shares") of the stock of ___Scrupulous Corporation___ (the "Corporation"). The Shares were represented by stock certificate number _____000009_____ issued on ___May 1, 1995___ (the "Certificate").

2. The undersigned is the sole owner of the Shares, having never endorsed, delivered, transferred, assigned, or otherwise disposed of them or the Certificate in such a way as to give any other person any interest in the Shares.

3. The undersigned has duly searched for the Certificate, has been unable to find it, and believes the Certificate to be lost, destroyed, or stolen.

4. In order to induce the Corporation to issue a new stock certificate to replace the Certificate, the undersigned agrees to indemnify, defend, and hold harmless the Corporation, its shareholders, directors, and officers from any and all claims, loss, or damage whatsoever arising out of or related in any manner to the Certificate or arising out of the issuance of a replacement certificate.

Dated:___September 5, 1997___

Hugh Hardy
_____
Hugh Hardy

STATE OF
COUNTY OF

On ___September 5,___, ___1997___, there personally appeared before me, _____Hugh Hardy_____, who ❏ is personally known to me ☒ produced ___New York driver's license___ as identification, and being duly sworn on oath stated that the facts stated in the above Affidavit are true.

John Galt
_____
John Galt
Notary Public

My Commission Expires: June 30, 1999

SHAREHOLDERS MEETINGS 5

LIVING WITH SHAREHOLDERS

The relationship among the officers, directors and shareholders of corporations varies from outright hostility to absolute unity of purpose. Remarkably, the law accommodates all these varied relationships, allowing cooperation where it is possible and remedies where they are necessary. The dynamics of the relationships vary with the number of shareholders.

SHAREHOLDERS AND CLOSE CORPORATIONS

Close corporations are small in the sense that they have few shareholders. What makes them close is that the shareholders, being few in number, are able to take a close interest in the business. Usually the shareholders are also directors or officers or both. Often they are all members of the same family. Disputes among the shareholders, officers and directors of close corporations are frequent enough, but usually they take the form of warring camps within a family, literally or figuratively. There is little opportunity for the officers or directors as groups to ally themselves against the shareholders because the relationships are too intertwined.

Most state laws allow for special treatment of close corporations. Some corporate statutes regulate them as a separate category. Others govern all corporations by the same set of rules, but allow smaller corporations to adopt rules recognizing their special circumstances. The MBCA, for example, allows corporations with fifty or fewer shareholders to dispense with the board of directors [MBCA, Sec. 8.01(c)] and give its function to the shareholders directly.

SHAREHOLDERS
AND LARGER
CORPORATIONS

Between close corporations and the corporate giants of the world are a great many medium sized corporations. Shareholder relationships often seem most difficult in these companies. They are too large to allow the shareholders to feel that they are in direct control and yet not so large that the shareholders feel unable to have any influence. They are difficult from a regulatory standpoint, too. Medium sized corporations are often on the edge between the loose regulation applied to privately owned companies and the much more stringent regulation burdening publicly owned companies. Too frequently the regulatory burden falls heavily on medium sized companies which often feel too strapped for cash to hire expensive lawyers. A lot of the regulatory burden has to do with shareholder relationships—raising capital and keeping shareholders adequately informed. If shareholder relations are hostile, the danger of expensive litigation is high.

SHAREHOLDERS
VERY LARGE
CORPORATIONS

A corporation with a very large number of shareholders is likely under the effective control of its officers and directors. There may be a few influential shareholders, but the great majority of shareholders never attend a shareholders meeting or even meet the people in control. The U.S. Securities and Exchange Commission will regulate shareholder relations in such a corporation, but the corporation will have the legal staff and funds to deal with the regulators with minimum inconvenience.

This chapter is directed to close corporations and those on the smaller side of the medium-sized group.

WHEN TO HAVE SHAREHOLDERS MEETINGS

ACTION WITHOUT MEETINGS

Don't forget that any action that can be taken by the shareholders in a meeting can be taken without a meeting by written consent (see chapter 1).

ANNUAL MEETINGS

The law requires one shareholders meeting a year and calls it the *annual meeting*. Although the meeting is required, failure to hold it on the date specified in the bylaws is not a serious problem for smaller corporations. You can hold it on a different date and call it the *substitute annual meeting*. If a year passes without such a meeting, the shareholders are entitled to complain and force a meeting by going to court.

Often bylaws will set a specific date every year on which the annual meeting is to be held. Frequently the date is inconvenient and must be changed. If it is, the meeting, whenever held, is properly called a substitute annual meeting. A more convenient arrangement is for the bylaws to allow the directors some flexibility in choosing the date of the annual meeting. The date should be a sufficient amount of time after the close of the fiscal year to allow the financial reports for the year to be completed and distributed to the shareholders before the meeting. Thus, most annual meetings are held in the spring, after the close of the fiscal year on the preceding December 31.

The date for the annual meeting as set in the bylaws may be changed by amending the bylaws. On the following page is a resolution amending the bylaws to allow for a flexible meeting date such as is discussed in the paragraph above. Next is a directors' resolution setting a specific date, time and place for the annual meeting within the period allowed by the amended bylaws. Most bylaws already allow flexibility as to the time and location of the meeting; although, a few require the meeting to be held at the company's principle offices.

The second example may also be modified to set the time and place for a substitute annual meeting by inserting the word "substitute" as appropriate.

R-20. **Resolution for amendment to the bylaws changing the date for the annual meeting—**

RESOLVED, that Article **[article number]**, Section **[section number]** of the bylaws of the corporation is hereby amended to read in its entirety as follows:

"The annual meeting of the shareholders shall be held on any day of the month of **[month]** of each year as may be determined by the board of directors."

R-21. **Resolution setting the time and place of the annual meeting—**

RESOLVED, that, pursuant to Article **[article number]**, Section **[section number]**, of the bylaws of the corporation, the annual meeting of shareholders shall take place at **[time of day]** on the **[date]** day of **[month]** at **[location]**, and further

RESOLVED, that the appropriate officers of the corporation are authorized and directed to give such notice of the meeting to shareholders of record on **[record date]** as may be required by law the bylaws of the corporation.

SPECIAL
MEETINGS

The company may also call a shareholders meeting at any time and for whatever purpose may be useful. Officers and directors usually don't enjoy the process of planning and conducting shareholders meetings, so extra ones are rare. If an item of business can wait for the next annual meeting, it probably will. Sometimes it can't wait. For example, if the company is merging with another company, the board of directors is likely to call a special meeting.

The statutes and probably your bylaws will allow a variety of people to call such meetings. If only the board of directors could do it, other than the annual meeting, there would be no way for the shareholders to meet and discuss the bad job being done by the board of directors. The following three examples are calls for meetings made by the directors, the President, and a group of shareholders representing more than 10% of the outstanding shares of the corporation. Form 28 is a call made by the President, and Form 29 is a call made by a group of shareholders.

> **R-22.** **Directors' resolution calling for a special shareholders meeting—**
>
> RESOLVED, that, pursuant to Article [article number], Section [section number], of the bylaws of the corporation, a special meeting of shareholders shall take place at [time of day] on the [date] day of [month] at [location], and further
>
> RESOLVED, that the purpose for which such meeting is called [is/are]:
>
> **[state the matters to be discussed and decided at the special meeting]**
>
> and further
>
> RESOLVED, that the appropriate officers of the corporation are authorized and directed to give such notice of the meeting to shareholders of record on [record date] as may be required by law and bylaws of the corporation.

Special shareholders meeting called by the president—

President's Call for Special Meeting of the Shareholders

To the Secretary of ___Scrupulous Corporation___

Pursuant to Article __8__, Section __2__ of the bylaws of the Corporation, there is hereby called a special meeting of the shareholders of the Corporation to be held on __March 22, 1997__, at __10:00__ a.m., at __the corporation's conference room__,
for the following purpose(s): discussion and vote on whether new warehouse should be purchased.

You are hereby authorized and directed to give such notice of the meeting to shareholders of record on __March 1, 1997__ as may be required by law and the bylaws of the Corporation.

Dated: _February 23, 1997_

Raymond Rodriguez

Raymond Rodriguez
President

Special shareholders meeting called by a group of shareholders—

Shareholder's Call for Special Meeting of the Shareholders

To the Secretary of Scrupulous Corporation

     Pursuant to Article ___8___, Section ___2___ of the bylaws of the Corporation, the undersigned shareholders of Scrupulous Corporation ,
representing not less than one-tenth of the shares entitled to vote on the issues described below, hereby call a special meeting of the shareholders of the Corporation to be held on March 22, 1997 , at 10:00 a .m., at _____
 the corporation's conference room ,
for the following purpose(s):

          to fill a vacancy on the board of directors

     You are hereby authorized and directed to give such notice of the meeting to shareholders of record on March 1, 1997 as may be required by law and the bylaws of the Corporation.

Dated: February 23, 1997

Henry Hardy
Henry Hardy; 10,000 shares

Calvin Collier
Calvin Collier; 2,500 shares

NOTICE OF MEETINGS

Notice of shareholders meetings. Unless the right is waived (using Form 33, which will be discussed later), shareholders must have written notice of any meeting held. The corporate secretary usually is responsible for making sure the notice is sent. If the secretary fails or refuses to do so, which sometimes happens when the meeting is called by the President or a group of disgruntled shareholders, the person or group responsible for calling the meeting may send out the notice.

RECORD DATE

The ownership of many large corporations changes constantly. The ownership of a close corporation may never change. Where change is constant, there must be some way of deciding which of the shareholders will get notice. For that reason a convenient date is chosen and shareholders of record on that *record date* are given notice. Of course, it may be that someone who is a shareholder on that date may not be a shareholder when the meeting comes around. If that is the case, the owner on the record date may simply give a proxy to the new shareholder so that he or she can vote the recently transferred shares.

Corporations used to "close the books" on the record date and not record any transfers between that date and the date of the meeting, but that is now a rare practice.

The bylaws may provide rules for selecting the record date. If not, the MBCA allows the directors to choose a date within limits (MBCA, Sec. 7.07). The statute and bylaws probably have a default record date if the directors fail to select one. The default date in the MBCA [Sec. 7.05(d)] is the close of business the day before the first notice is given to shareholders. For close corporations where shares are seldom if ever transferred, this default date is usually sufficient.

NOTICE OF ANNUAL MEETING

Usually, the notice of an annual meeting need not state the particular matters to be discussed; although, many corporations do so nevertheless.

There are some exceptions, however. Some matters (mergers and the like) are of such fundamental importance to the corporation that the shareholders are entitled to notice whenever such issues are up for a decision. If any matter other than the ordinary election of directors is to be discussed and voted on at an annual meeting, it would be wise to see your lawyer to make sure notice is adequate. If the corporation is regulated by the Securities and Exchange Commission, the regulations require that substantial information be sent along with the notice, but companies regulated by the Securities and Exchange Commission are beyond the scope of this book.

Your bylaws will have a provision setting a window of time within which notice must be sent. The MBCA requires you to give notice not less than ten nor more than sixty days before the meeting [MBCA, Sec. 7.05(a)].

Form 30 is a form of notice for an annual meeting. The same form may be used for a substitute annual meeting by inserting the word "substitute" as appropriate. Below is an example of such a notice:

Notice of the annual shareholders' meeting—

Notice of Annual Meeting of the Shareholders of
Scrupulous Corporation

Date: April 3, 1997

TO: All Shareholders

The annual meeting of the shareholders of the Corporation will be a special meeting of the board of directors on April 24 , 1997 , at 11:00 a .m., at Dewey, Cheatham & Howe, 420 East 59th St., Ste. 2416 New York, NY .

The purposes of the meeting are:

1.   To elect directors.

2.   To transact such business as may properly come before the meeting and any adjournment or adjournments thereof.

By order of the board of directors:

Roberta Moore

Roberta Moore
Corporate Secretary

NOTICE OF
SPECIAL
MEETINGS

The significant difference between the notice required for special meetings and that required for annual meetings is that, for special meetings, the purpose of the meeting must be described. The above warning about companies regulated by the Securities and Exchange Commission applies here as well. Form 31 is a notice for a special meeting, and below is a completed example:

Notice of a special shareholders' meeting—

Notice of Special Meeting of the Shareholders of

Scrupulous Corporation

Date: April 3, 1997

TO: All Shareholders

A special meeting of the shareholders of the Corporation will be held on April 24 , 1997 , at 11:00 a.m., at Dewey, Cheatham & Howe, 420 East 59th St., Ste. 2416, New York, NY .

The purposes of the meeting are:

Discuss and vote on merger with Honor Corporation.

(Lunch at The Pizza Palace will follow meeting.)

By order of the board of directors:

Roberta Moore

Roberta Moore
Corporate Secretary

SECRETARY'S
AFFIDAVIT

The law requires that notice be sent; not that the secretary sign an affidavit to that effect. However, sometimes disputes about the validity of a corporate action may arise months or years after it is taken. A written record that the proper notice was given can be a life saver. Form 32 provides such a record. It should be kept in the corporate minute book along with the minutes of the meeting. The odd phrase "caused…to be deposited" covers the likelihood that the Secretary didn't actually mail the notice, but ordered it done. Below is an example:

Secretary's affidavit regarding mailing of notice—

Affidavit of Mailing

The undersigned, being duly sworn, hereby affirms the following:

1.   I am the Corporate Secretary of __Scrupulous Corporation__ _____ (the "Corporation").

2.   On __May 18, 1997__, I caused notice of the __annual__ meeting of the shareholders of the Corporation to be deposited in the United States Post Office at __New York, NY_____, in sealed envelopes, postage prepaid, addressed to each shareholder of the Corporation of record on __May 15, 1997__ at his or her last known address as it appeared on the books of the Corporation.

3.   A copy of such notice is attached to and incorporated by reference into this affidavit.

Date: __May 19, 1997__

Roberta Moore
_____
Roberta Moore
Secretary

STATE OF   New York
COUNTY OF   Jamaica

On _____ __May 19__ , __1997__ , there personally appeared before me, __Roberta Moore_____, who, being duly sworn, deposed and said that he/she is the Secretary of __Scrupulous Corporation__, and that the facts stated in the above Affidavit are true.

John Galt
_____
John Galt
Notary Public
My Commission Expires: June 30, 1999

WAIVER OF
NOTICE

Like notice of a directors meeting (see chapter 3), the notice of a shareholders meeting may be waived. Waivers should be kept with the minutes of the meeting. If notice is not required, of course it need not be waived. So mention of an annual meeting in Form 33 is only for those annual meetings which include matters for which notice is required by statute. If you are doing any such thing, you should be in contact with your lawyer. Below is an example of a waiver:

Shareholder's waiver of notice—

Shareholder's Waiver of Notice

The undersigned Shareholder(s) of _____ Scrupulous Corporation _____
_____ hereby waive any and all notice required
by law or by the articles of incorporation or bylaws of the Corporation and consent to
the holding of ❑ the annual ☒ a special meeting of the shareholders of the
corporation on _____ June 18, 1997 _____ at ___ 7:00 ___ _p_.m., at
the corporation's headquarters conference room
for the following purposes:

Election of directors and any other matters.

Raymond Rodriguez   Date: _6/18/97_
Shareholder

Henry Hardy   Date: _6/18/97_
Shareholder

Calvin Collier   Date: _June 18, 1997_
Shareholder

Della Driskell   Date: _6/18/97_
Shareholder

_____   Date: _____
Shareholder

_____   Date: _____
Shareholder

PLANNING AND CONDUCTING MEETINGS

PREPARATION

Getting ready for a shareholders meeting is not a welcome task, but it is an important one. In the corporate giants of the world, there are people whose job descriptions include planning the annual meeting. In smaller companies the job falls to people who already have a desk full of things to do and are therefore tempted to cut corners. But shareholder relations are often more sensitive in the smaller companies than the larger, so avoid the temptation if you can. It may be the only chance you have to meet your shareholders, and the bad news is that a lot of shareholders don't go to annual meetings at all unless they are already unhappy. Never forget that the company (or at least the people who run the company) is on display. Your good attitude and careful preparation may soothe a concerned shareholder. An attitude that gives the shareholders the impression that the meeting is only a necessary inconvenience may give the shareholders the idea that that's what you think of them, too.

Unless you know for sure that the meeting will be uneventful and the shareholders docile, it may be a good idea to have your lawyer there. If you know there will be angry shareholders present or that there is a possibility of cumulative voting (see below), you definitely should. Always remember that the shareholders are taking what you say seriously. One CEO was carefully warned by his lawyer that even informal predictions or representations made at a meeting might be held against the CEO later, if some shareholder bought or sold shares relying on that information. At the meeting, the CEO, understandably excited about the company's prospects, found it hard not to predict the future. In front of the assembled shareholders, he turned to the lawyer and asked, "Can I speak off the record?" The lawyer said "No" (there were stronger words to follow after the meeting). You are responsible for what you say. By forgetting that and asking the lawyer's permission to ignore his advice, the CEO had inadvertently given the shareholders the impression that maybe what he was saying was in some way not reliable.

Most bylaws allow the meeting to be held at any place the directors choose. Officers and directors are likely to choose the place most convenient for them. That may be, but is not necessarily, the best choice. If there is room for the meeting at the company offices, and you are enthusiastic or at least content to allow the shareholders to have a close look at the operation, then it's a good location. If you can't make a good impression, or if the shareholders would be uncomfortable there, think about a meeting room off the premises.

An agenda for any meeting is a good idea. It does not have to be distributed to the shareholders, but may be. Form 34 is an agenda form.

A *script* is what each person will say at the meeting, word-for-word. A script looks unnecessarily elaborate, but can be very important, especially if the person presiding is uncomfortable being in charge of formal meetings. It can make the meeting appear more "professional" to the shareholders attending the meeting. It should be distributed to anyone with a part to play. Below are examples of an agenda and a script for a meeting. Your bylaws may designate a person, usually the President or the Chairman of the Board, to preside at shareholders meetings. Usually the bylaws allow that person to designate an alternate.

Agenda for a shareholders meeting—

Agenda of Meeting of the Shareholders of

Scrupulous Corporation

Date of Meeting: June 18, 1997

1. Call to order and welcome of shareholders and guests by the President.
2. Announcement regarding call of meeting, notice, and presence of a quorum by the Secretary.
3. Report on business developments since the last share holders' meeting and discussion of financial statements.
4. Election of directors.
5. Ratification of independent accountants.
6. [Other matters specified in the notice.]
7. Other matters.
8. Adjournment.

Script of a shareholders meeting—

```
                          Script
            Annual Meeting of Shareholders
                 Scrupulous Corporation
            Date of Meeting: June 18, 1997
```

PRESIDENT: The annual meeting of the shareholders of Scrupulous Corporation is called to order. My name is Raymond Rodriguez and I am President of the Company. I would very much like to welcome all of our shareholders. It is a pleasure to have you here at the company's offices, and I hope your visit is enjoyable.

We have some other distinguished guests here today that I would like to recognize. I will ask each to stand and be recognized, but for the sake of time, I ask you to hold any applause until the last introduction is complete.

First is a representative of our independent accountants, [Mr./Ms. Name]. of the firm of [Firm name], who will be available throughout the meeting to answer any questions you may have about the financial statements you have received.

Next is [Mr./Ms. Name] of the law firm [Firm name] our company attorney.

Next I am pleased to introduce the members of the board of directors who are present and who have contributed in a very significant way to the company's success during the last year: [Names of board members].

Seated next to me are the Chief Financial Officer of the Company, [Mr./Ms. Name] and the Secretary of the Company, [Mr./Ms. Name] who will be speaking to you in a moment.

Finally, we are pleased to have as a special guest here [Mr./Ms. Name] who was the company's top salesperson for the past year. I hope you will have an opportunity to meet and offer your personal thanks to [First Name] for the outstanding job [he/she] and the other company employees have done this past year.

I now ask the Secretary to report on the call of the meeting.

SECRETARY: Thank you, [Mr./Ms.] President. Pursuant to the bylaws of the corporation, the board of directors, by resolution adopted [Date] called this annual meeting of the shareholders of [Name of corporation] and established [Record date] as the record date for the determination of shareholders entitled to notice of and to vote at this meeting.

Notice of the meeting was mailed to the shareholders of record on [Date]. My affidavit regarding the mailing is on file with the company.

An alphabetical list of the shareholders and their addresses and number of shares held by each as of the record date is available at this meeting for reference and has been available for inspection for the period required by the bylaws of the Company.

Of the [Number of outstanding shares] shares of common stock of the company outstanding on the record date, shareholders holding [Number of shares represented at the meeting] are present at this meeting in person or by proxy. This number represents [Percentage of outstanding shares represented at the meeting] which number constitutes a quorum for the transaction of business.

PRESIDENT: Thank you, [Name]. A quorum being present, I declare this meeting duly constituted for the transaction of all business. Before we begin the matters to be voted on by shareholders, I would like to ask [Mr./Ms. Name], our Chief Financial Officer to briefly report on developments of the past year.

CFO: [CFO's report. Questions from the shareholders regarding report.]

PRESIDENT: Thank you, [Name]. [Additional comments by the President on the CFO's report or the Company generally.]

Next we go to the items to be voted on by shareholders. The nominating committee of your board of directors has nominated all of the current board members to stand for reelection. All of the members have served in that capacity for some time, and I believe you are familiar with their qualifications and their excellent service.

Voting for the directors today will be by ballot. I believe you were given a ballot when you arrived at the meeting, but if any more are needed, please let me know now. [Pause to distribute additional ballots if necessary.] I now ask if there are any other nominations for the board of directors from the shareholders present at the meeting.

PRESELECTED SHAREHOLDER #1: I move that the nominations for directors be closed.

PRESELECTED SHAREHOLDER #2: I second the motion.

PRESIDENT: Will those in favor of closing the nominations please so indicate. [Pause] Will those opposed please so indicate.

[Pause] The motion is carried, and nominations for directors of the corporation are closed.

I now ask that you mark your ballots in the spaces provided. When you are finished they will be collected and counted. [Pause for voting]

While the votes are being counted, I suggest that we proceed to the next matter to be decided, the ratification of [Firm name] as the company's independent auditors. I offer the following resolution:

"RESOLVED, that the appointment by the board of directors of [Firm name], Certified Public Accountants, as independent auditors for the company in connection with the fiscal year ended [Ending date of the current fiscal year] is hereby approved, ratified and confirmed."

SHAREHOLDER #1: I move that the resolution presented regarding the appointment of independent auditors be adopted.

SHAREHOLDER #2: I second the motion.

PRESIDENT: Voting on the resolution presented will be by voice vote. All those in favor of adopting the resolution presented please so indicate. [Pause] All those opposed please so indicate. [Pause] Hearing no votes in opposition to the motion, I declare the motion duly adopted.

[Disposition of other matters specified in the meeting notice.]

I now ask the Secretary to report on the results of the election of directors.

SECRETARY: [Mr./Ms.] President, each of the nominees for director has received at least [Number in excess of majority] votes which is in excess of the number required for election.

PRESIDENT: Thank you. Each having received a number of votes exceeding that required for election, I declare the nominees for director duly elected to serve as directors.

If there is no further business to come before the meeting, I would entertain a motion that the meeting be adjourned.

SHAREHOLDER #1: I move that the meeting be adjourned.

SHAREHOLDER #2: I second the motion.

PRESIDENT: All those in favor please so indicate. [Pause] All those opposed please so indicate. [Pause] Thanks to all of you for your presence and cooperation. I declare this meeting to be adjourned.

VOTING BY
PROXY

Unlike directors, shareholders don't have to cast their votes in person. A director is an elected servant of the corporation and accordingly owes the corporation his or her best personal judgment on the issues up for vote. A shareholder owns shares for his or her own interest and may chose whether to vote and how. More practically, if the thousands of shareholders of a corporate giant had to personally attend meetings in order to vote, there would never be a quorum and no decisions could be made.

A shareholder's "absentee ballot" is called a proxy form. It's not really an absentee ballot, of course. It is a kind of power of attorney in which the shareholder appoints an agent to attend the meeting and cast the shareholder's vote. The shareholder may allow the proxy unlimited discretion to decide how the vote should be cast or may tell the proxy exactly how the vote must be cast.

Like the buying and selling of stock, all voting by proxy is regulated to some degree by the U.S. Securities and Exchange Commission and by state regulators. Anyone who "solicits a proxy" (that is, talks a shareholder into giving his or her proxy to the person asking for it) using false or misleading information is guilty of a kind of fraud and is subject to severe penalties. Anyone who solicits more than a very few proxies to vote the shares of a corporation, and the management of companies with large numbers of shareholders, may be subject to very elaborate reporting and notification requirements which are beyond the scope of this book. For that reason, the following proxy forms are not intended to be used where a person seeks to gather multiple proxies in the hope of influencing the outcome of an election. However, they are appropriate where a shareholder, for the sake of convenience or necessity, wishes another person to cast the shareholder's vote under various circumstances.

Form 35 gives the proxy general voting powers for a period of time. It is usable at any shareholders meeting which occurs while it is in effect. Proxy forms are valid for 11 months unless another expiration date is given on the form [MBCA, Sec. 7.22(c)]. Form 36 appoints a proxy for just one meeting, and Form 37 does the same with specific instructions on how to vote.

Usually, the shareholder can revoke a proxy appointment at any time up to the moment a vote is cast. The exception is when it is "coupled with an interest," meaning that the proxy has some ownership interest (e.g., a security lien) or other contractual right specified by statute [MBCA Sec. 7.22(d)].

The phrase "with full power of substitution" means the proxy may appoint a substitute proxy. The forms below do not deal with the possibility of cumulative voting (see discussion below). If cumulative voting is reasonably likely to occur, specific instructions should be added to the proxy form as appropriate. Examples of Forms 35, 36 and 37 follow:

Proxy (general)—

Appointment of Proxy

The undersigned Shareholder (the "Shareholder") of _____ Scrupulous Corporation _____ (the "Corporation") hereby appoints _____ Hugh Hardy _____ as proxy, with full power of substitution, for and in the name of the Shareholder to attend all shareholders meetings of the Corporation and to act, vote, and execute consents with respect to any or all shares of the Corporation belonging to the Shareholder as fully and to the same extent and effect as the Shareholder. This appointment may be revoked by the Shareholder at any time; but, if not revoked, shall continue in effect until _March 31, 1998_____.

The date of this proxy is _October 3, 1997_____.

_Henry Hardy_____
Shareholder

Proxy (particular meeting)—

Appointment of Proxy

The undersigned Shareholder (the "Shareholder") of _____
_____ Scrupulous Corporation _____ (the "Corporation") hereby
appoints _____ Hugh Hardy _____ as proxy, with full
power of substitution, for and in the name of the Shareholder to attend the
❏ annual   ☒ special shareholders' meeting of the Corporation to be held on
October 12, 1997 _____, at __ 7:00 _____ p .m., at ___ the corporation's
__ headquarters conference room _____, and to act and vote at
such meeting and any adjournment thereof with respect to any or all shares of the
Corporation belonging to the Shareholder as fully and to the same extent and effect as
the Shareholder. Any appointment of proxy previously made by the Shareholder for
such meeting is hereby revoked.

The date of this proxy is _ October 3, 1997 _____.

Henry Hardy _____
Shareholder

Proxy (specific action)—

Appointment of Proxy

The undersigned Shareholder (the "Shareholder") of _____
_____ Scrupulous Corporation _____(the "Corporation") hereby
appoints _____ Hugh Hardy _____ as proxy, with full
power of substitution, for and in the name of the Shareholder to attend the
❏ annual   ☒ special shareholders' meeting of the Corporation to be held on
_____ October 12, 1997 _____, at 7:00 _____ _ p .m., at _____ the corporation's
__ headquarters conference room _____, and to act and vote at
such meeting and any adjournment thereof with respect to any or all shares of the
Corporation belonging to the Shareholder as directed below and in his or her discretion
as to any other business that may properly come before the meeting or any adjournment:

To vote on filling the current vacancy on the board of directors, and
to vote for the purchase of a building for new corporate offices.

Any appointment of proxy previously made by the Shareholder for such meeting
is hereby revoked.

The date of this proxy is _ October 3, 1997 _____.

Calvin Collier _____
Shareholder

CUMULATIVE
VOTING

Shareholder elections are a fairly harsh version of democracy. The majority rules, and there is not much in the way of a "Bill of Rights" for the minority. Usually, if you control fifty-one percent of the outstanding shares, you get to choose all the directors. There are some curbs on this majority tyranny. One of them is *cumulative* voting. Under this system, each shareholder multiplies the number of shares he or she controls times the number of directors up for election. The result is the number of votes each shareholder may cast, and he or she may spread them around in any way that pleases—all for one nominee, equally among all nominees, etc. If you own enough shares, and the math works out, you may be able to elect at least one director by yourself even though you own less than a majority of all the shares.

Not every corporation allows its shareholders this right. It depends on state law and the articles of incorporation. If your corporation allows cumulative voting and you think some shareholder may invoke that right at an upcoming meeting, it would be doubly wise to invite your lawyer to the meeting. The vote counting can be a nightmare and it frequently comes up when the shareholder invoking the right is already angry at the current board of directors. Voting by ballot (see below) in a cumulative voting election is practically essential.

BALLOT VOTING

Some states require that shareholder votes be cast by ballot rather than by voice vote or some other means. Elsewhere it is optional. For corporations with more than a handful of shareholders, in matters where there is any substantial disagreement, it is a practical necessity for two reasons: It provides a written record of how votes were cast, and it makes counting votes much easier. Regarding the latter, think of the situation where you have three shareholders sitting in a row. One owns ten shares, one owns fifty, and the third 100. Two shareholders vote "yes" and one votes "no." Has the issue passed? Unless you can look at each shareholder and tell how many shares he or she owns, you don't know.

Form 38 is a shareholder ballot that might be used in that election of directors. An example follows on the next page.

Shareholder ballot—

Shareholder Ballot

Annual Shareholders Meeting of

Scrupulous Corporation

Held on: April 7, 1997

The undersigned shareholder and/or proxy holder votes the shares described below as follows:

FOR ELECTION OF DIRECTORS:

	Name of director	Shares voted for	Shares voted against
1.	Henry Hardy	150	0
2.	Raymond Rodriguez	150	0
3.	Della Driskell	150	0
4.	Calvin Collier	100	50
5.	Hugh Hardy	150	0
6.	Roberta Moore	150	0

Number of shares voted by the undersigned in person: 850
Number of shares voted by the undersigned as proxy: 50
Total shares voted by this ballot: 900

A copy of the proxy form(s) authorizing the undersigned to vote by proxy as above is attached to this ballot.

Hugh Hardy
(signature)

Hugh Hardy
(name printed)

KEEPING
RECORDS

The minutes of the shareholders meeting are the official memory of what happened. See the discussion of minutes in chapter 1. Below is an example of minutes (Form 5 and Form 7).

Minutes of a shareholders' meeting—

Minutes of the Annual Meeting of the Shareholders of

Scrupulous Corporation

The annual meeting of the Shareholders of the Corporation was held on the date and at the time and place set forth in the written notice of meeting, or waiver of notice signed by shareholders, and attached to the minutes of this meeting.

The following shareholders were present:

Shareholder	No. of Shares
Henry Hardy	20,000
Raymond Rodriguez	15,000
Della Driskell	15,000
Calvin Collier	15,000
Hugh Hardy	20,000
Roberta Moore	15,000

The meeting was called to order and it was moved, seconded and carried that _____ Raymond Rodriguez act as Chairman and that Roberta Moore act as Secretary.

A roll call was taken and the Chairman noted that all of the outstanding shares of the Corporation were represented in person or by proxy. Any proxies are attached to these minutes.

Minutes of the preceding meeting of the Shareholders, held on January 7, 1997, were read and approved.

Upon motion duly made, seconded and carried, the following were elected directors for the following year:

Calvin Collier	Hugh Hardy
Della Driskell	Roberta Moore

The President welcomed those present and introduced the following guests:

Representing Bean-Counter Associates: Tex A. Voydence
Representing Dewey, Cheatham & Howe: Sue M. Goode

(See Continuation Sheets)

There being no further business, the meeting adjourned.

Roberta Moore
Secretary

Approved:
Raymond Rodriguez

Shareholders Meeting Minutes Continuation Sheet

Type & Date of Meeting:___Annual Meeting, April 7, 1997_____

Page_____ of _____ pages.

The President announced that the representative of Bean-Counter Associates would be available to answer any questions that might arise regarding the company's financial statements.

The Secretary then announced that the meeting had been called by resolution of the directors on January 14, 1997, and that notice of the meeting had been mailed as detailed in the Secretary's affidavit, a copy of which is attached to these minutes and incorporated herein by reference. She stated that, of the 100,000 shares of common shares outstanding, 100,000 shares were represented at the meeting in person or by proxy and that a quorum was therefore present.

The President declared the meeting duly constituted for the transaction of business and called on the Chief Financial Officer to report on recent developments in the Company. A summary of the CFO's report is available in the corporation's main business office. After the report, the CFO and the President entertained brief questions from the shareholders present.

The President announced that the Nominating Committee of the board of directors had nominated the current directors for reelection and that voting for directors would be by ballot. Ballots distributed to the shareholders contained the names of each of the current directors, that is: Della Driskell, Hugh hardy, Calvin Collier, and Roberta Moore.

The President asked if there were additional nominations from the floor. Henry Hardy moved that nominations for director be closed, and the motions was seconded by Raymond Rodriguez. The motion was approved by voice vote, and the President declared the nominations closed.

The President invited the shareholders to complete their ballots and, while the votes were counted, proceeded to the next order of business, the ratification of the company's independent auditors.

"RESOLVED, that the appointment by the board of directors of Bean-Counter Associates, Certified Public Accountants, as independent auditors for the company in connection with the fiscal year ended February 28, 1997, is hereby approved, ratified and confirmed."

Shareholders Meeting Minutes Continuation Sheet

Type & Date of Meeting: <u>Annual Meeting, April 7, 1997</u>

Page <u>3</u> of <u>3</u> pages.

 Henry Hardy moved that the resolution be adopted, and the motion was seconded by Raymond Rodriguez. The resolution was approved by voice vote, and the President declared that it was duly adopted.

 The President then asked the Secretary to report on the results of the election of directors. The Secretary stated that each of the nominees had received more than a majority of those shares present and entitled to vote, and the President declared that each of the nominees listed above were duly elected. The ballots submitted and counted in the elections for director are located at the regular business office of the corporation.

Also as in the case of minutes of directors meetings, corporate secretaries are occasionally asked to produce official copies of the minutes. Form 11 and Form 12 are for certification of the minutes. For certification of a particular resolution adopted by shareholders, use Form 13 or Form 14). The following are examples of these two forms:

Secretary's certification of the minutes of a shareholders meeting—

Certified Copy of Minutes of Meeting of the Shareholders of

<u>Scrupulous Corporation</u>

I HEREBY CERTIFY that I am the Corporate Secretary of <u>   </u> <u>Scrupulous Corporation</u>, that the attached is an accurate copy of the minutes of the meeting of the Shareholders of the corporation, held on <u>April 7</u>, <u>1997</u>.
Signed and the seal of the Corporation affixed, <u>July 20</u>, <u>1997</u>.

<u>*Roberta Moore*</u>
Roberta Moore
Secretary

Secretary's certification of a particular resolution adopted by the shareholders—

Certified Copy of Resolutions Adopted by the Shareholders of

Scrupulous Corporation

    I HEREBY CERTIFY that I am the Corporate Secretary of _____ Scrupulous Corporation _____, that the following is an accurate copy of resolution(s) adopted by the Shareholders of the corporation, effective _____ April 7 _____, ___ 1997 __, and that such resolutions continue in effect as of the date of this certification:

"RESOLVED, that the appointment by the board of directors of Bean-Counter Associates, Certified Public Accountants, as independent auditors for the company in connection with the fiscal year ended February 28, 1997, is hereby approved, ratified and confirmed."

    Signed and the seal of the Corporation affixed, _____ July 20 _____, __ 1997 __.

Roberta Moore
Roberta Moore
Secretary

DIVIDENDS 6

ACCOUNTING ISSUES—
IS THERE ENOUGH MONEY FOR A DIVIDEND?

States have tried various financial tests for a corporation to determine whether it has enough cash or assets or both to safely declare and pay a dividend. The MBCA (Sec. 6.40) forbids a dividend if, after the dividend is paid, the company cannot pay its debts as they become due, or if its liabilities are greater than its assets. For this purpose, liabilities include preferences owed to any preferred shareholders if the company were dissolved. Check with your accountant.

The calculation may not be as straightforward as you imagine and the penalties for a director who votes for an illegal dividend—one that doesn't meet the test—are severe. The director may be personally liable for restoring the money to the corporation.

Dividends need not be paid in cash. They can be paid in property belonging to the corporation or in corporate shares.

THE ROLE OF DIRECTORS IN DECLARING DIVIDENDS

A right to receive a share of the company's profits is one of the basic rights of shareholders. You might think that it would be something the shareholders could vote on, but they can't. Only the board of directors can declare a dividend for fear that, given the power to raid the corporate treasury, the shareholders might take more than is wise.

RECORD DATE

As is the case with deciding who is entitled to vote shares of stock, there must be a way of determining who are the shareholders entitled to receive a dividend. The list is established as of a record date chosen by the directors. See chapter 5.

CASH DIVIDENDS —COMMON STOCK

Common shareholders have a right as shareholders to share in the company's profits, but they don't have a right to a particular dividend. They only get a dividend when the directors decide it is time and pass a resolution declaring one. This the directors can do at irregular intervals. Many companies establish a policy of declaring regular dividends which the shareholders come to rely on. Nevertheless, the directors are free to forego a *regular dividend* if they wish simply by not declaring it. The following are two resolutions, one where the directors establish a policy of regular dividend payments, and one where a single dividend is declared:

R-23. **Directors' resolution establishing a regular quarterly cash dividend (common stock)—**

RESOLVED, that to the extent permitted by law, it is the intent of the board of directors that the corporation shall henceforth pay regular quarterly dividends on the common shares of the corporation in the amount of $[amount] per share of common stock issued and outstanding, and further

RESOLVED, that the declaration and payment of such regular dividends shall in every case be subject to the board's reasonable judgment as to their advisability at the time of such declaration.

> **R-24.** Directors' resolution declaring a cash dividend (common stock)—
>
> RESOLVED, that there is hereby declared a cash dividend on the common shares of the corporation in the amount of $[amount] per share issued and outstanding, payable on [payment date] to shareholders of record on [record date], and further
>
> RESOLVED, that the appropriate officers of the corporation are authorized and directed to take such actions as may be necessary or desirable to give effect to the foregoing resolution and to properly record the payment of such dividend in the accounts of the company.

CASH DIVIDENDS —PREFERRED STOCK

The dividends paid on preferred shares are usually expressed as a percentage of the issue price. For example, if preferred shares with an annual dividend of $1.00 were sold by the corporation for $10 per share, the shares have a 10% annual dividend ($1.00 per share per year is 10% of the $10.00 purchase price). The resolution declaring the first quarterly dividend on those shares would declare a dividend of $0.25, as in the example below. (Remember that even preferred dividends may not be paid until each dividend is declared by the board of directors.)

> **R-25.** Directors' resolution declaring a dividend on preferred shares—
>
> RESOLVED, that there is hereby declared the regular quarterly cash dividend on the preferred shares of the corporation in the amount of $[amount] per share issued and outstanding, payable on [payment date] to shareholders of record on [record date], and further
>
> RESOLVED, that the appropriate officers of the corporation are authorized and directed to take such actions as may be necessary or desirable to give effect to the foregoing resolution and to properly record the payment of such dividend in the accounts of the company.

STOCK
DIVIDENDS

Dividends payable in stock of the corporation, rather than in cash or other property, don't affect the ownership of the company. Each existing shareholder gets new shares of stock, and they are distributed among the shareholders pro rata. So if you own ten percent of the outstanding shares of the corporation before the stock dividend, you own ten percent after. There are just more shares outstanding. Why do it then? Shareholders of publicly traded corporations usually do see a slight increase in the total market value of their shares after a stock dividend. For small companies there is little reason to do it unless you just want there to be more outstanding shares. It is a simple process, provided there are enough shares authorized in the articles of incorporation. If there are not enough authorized, then the articles must be amended by the shareholders to increase the number authorized. Because the shareholders don't own any more after the stock dividend than they did before, it should have no income tax effect.

A stock split may have the same effect as a stock dividend, but it is conceptually different. The effect is that the shareholders own more shares than they did before, but their percentage ownership of the company doesn't change. But rather than new shares being issued, the old outstanding shares are divided or *split* by some factor so that there are more than there were. Again there is no tax effect.

The mechanism for effecting a split is more complicated than that for a stock dividend in most states. If the shares are par value shares, usually the articles of incorporation must be amended to reduce the par value. If the shares are *no par*, an amendment may not be necessary, depending on whether state law requires the articles to include the "stated capital per share."

Logically, a reverse stock split is the opposite. The old outstanding shares become fewer. If a stock split or reverse stock split involves a change in par value, it may be advisable to retrieve the old share certificates (because they will state the old par value) and replace them with new certificates.

If your company is in need of a stock split or reverse stock split (or if you don't have enough authorized shares for a stock dividend), you should consult your lawyer and accountant about the undoubtedly unique factors that will affect the process.

Below is an example of a resolution declaring a stock dividend:

R-26.   Directors' resolution declaring a stock dividend—

RESOLVED, that there is hereby declared a stock dividend on the common shares of the corporation at the rate of **[number]** share(s) of common stock for each share issued and outstanding, payable on **[payment date]** to shareholders of record on **[record date]**, and further

RESOLVED, that the appropriate officers of the corporation are authorized and directed to take such actions as may be necessary or desirable to issue new stock certificates, to otherwise give effect to the foregoing resolution and to properly record the payment of such dividend in the accounts of the company.

DIVIDENDS PAID IN PROPERTY OTHER THAN CASH OR SHARES OF THE COMPANY

Sometimes a corporation will own property that it would like to give to its shareholders. The way to do it is with a *dividend in kind*. The property could be anything from land to paper clips, but most frequently it is paid in stock of some company *other than* the company paying the dividend. For example, suppose your company owns a subsidiary it no longer wants. It could sell the subsidiary or it could "spin it off" by giving it to the shareholders. The following example of a resolution accomplishes such a dividend, but can be used for other kinds of property dividends by changing the description of the property as appropriate.

Unlike a stock dividend or split, a dividend in kind may have very significant tax effects.

R-27.   Directors' resolution declaring a dividend in kind—

RESOLVED, that there is hereby declared a dividend on the common shares of the corporation payable in shares of stock of **[name of subsidiary]** at the rate of **[number of shares]** of stock for each share of **[name of corporation declaring dividend]** issued and outstanding, payable on **[payment date]** to shareholders of record on **[record date]**, and further

RESOLVED, that the appropriate officers of the corporation are authorized and directed to take such actions as may be necessary or desirable to give effect to the foregoing resolution and to properly record the payment of such dividend in the accounts of the company.

OFFICERS 7

THE PLACE OF THE OFFICERS IN THE CORPORATION

Unlike shareholders and directors, officers *are* agents of the corporation and do represent the corporation with power to bind it in contractual relationships. They carry out their function as individuals rather than through group decisions. As "executives," they execute the policies of the directors.

NUMBER OF OFFICERS

How many officers does a corporation need? Modern corporate statutes allow wide flexibility in creating corporate offices. There is no requirement to have an officer bearing any specific title, although, there is little reason for a corporation to deviate from the standard list and many good reasons for sticking with it. The standard list includes a president, vice president and secretary. Often the secretary also holds the title and duties of the vice president and treasurer. It is common for one person to hold more than one office, but the same person should not be both president and secretary. Many documents require the signature of both and may not be signed twice by the same person.

State laws and contracting parties often presume (and in some cases require) that documents, notably deeds, will be signed by the president (or vice president) and attested (i.e., have the corporate seal attached) by the secretary. Any corporation will soon find that these two offices are a practical necessity. Any other arrangement, although legal, would require unending explanation and justification to outsiders. The next most useful office is that of an assistant secretary who can fill in to sign corporate documents when the secretary is not conveniently available.

Beyond these basics, the possibilities are endless. Corporations have invented any number of imaginative titles such as "first assistant vice president for public information."

DUTIES OF
OFFICERS

In addition to signing documents, the officers may be assigned a long list of general duties and, as agents of the company, may be assigned specific, temporary responsibilities as the need arises. The following five examples of bylaw provisions describe the standard duties for the officers indicated. They are written as they might appear in the company's bylaws or a resolution to amend the bylaws, but the same job descriptions might also be used to describe an officer's duties in an employment contract.

R-28.   Bylaw provision establishing the duties of the president—

The President shall be the chief executive officer of the corporation and, subject to the direction and control of the Board of Directors, shall supervise and manage the business affairs of the corporation and perform all duties incident to the office of President and other duties as may be assigned by the Board of Directors from time to time. The President shall have authority to sign, with the Secretary, an Assistant Secretary, or any other officer of the corporation duly authorized by the Board of Directors, share certificates of the corporation, deeds, deeds of trust, mortgages, bonds, contracts, or other instruments authorized by the Board of Directors to be executed by the corporation, unless authority to sign such instruments shall have been expressly delegated by the Board of Directors or required by law to be signed by some other officer or agent. The President shall, when present, preside at meetings of the Shareholders.

R-29. Bylaw provision establishing the duties of the vice president—

Any Vice President shall perform the duties of the President when the President is absent, unable or unwilling to act. When so acting, a Vice President shall have the same powers and be subject to the same limitations as the President. Any Vice President shall have authority to sign, with the Secretary, an Assistant Secretary, or any other officer of the corporation duly authorized by the Board of Directors, share certificates of the corporation, deeds, deeds of trust, mortgages, bonds, contracts, or other instruments authorized by the Board of Directors to be executed by the corporation, unless authority to sign such instruments shall have been expressly delegated by the Board of Directors or required by law to be signed by some other officer or agent. The Vice President shall also have and perform other duties as may be assigned by the Board of Directors from time to time.

R-30. Bylaw provision establishing the duties of the secretary—

The Secretary shall have such duties as may be assigned by the President or the Board of Directors from time to time and shall perform all duties incident to the office of Secretary including but not limited to the following: (1) Having custody and maintenance of the records of the corporation, including the stock transfer books, and authenticating the same when requested or required to do so. (2) Having custody of the seal of the corporation and affixing it to documents which are duly authorized to be executed under seal. (3) With the President or a Vice President, the signing of certificates for shares of the corporation, the issuance of which have been duly authorized. (4) Giving notice of all meetings of shareholders, directors and committees as required by law and the bylaws of the corporation. (5) Preparing minutes of all such meetings in properly organized and maintained books. (6) Preparing shareholder lists prior to each shareholders' meeting as required by law and the bylaws of the corporation.

R-31.   Bylaw provision establishing the duties of the assistant secretary—

Any Assistant Secretary shall perform the duties of the Secretary when the Secretary is absent, unable or unwilling to act. When so acting, an Assistant Secretary shall have the same powers and be subject to the same limitations as the Secretary. Any Assistant Secretary, with the President or a Vice President, may sign certificates for shares of the corporation, the issuance of which have been duly authorized. An Assistant Secretary shall perform such other duties as may be assigned by the President or the Board of Directors from time to time.

R-32.   Bylaw provision establishing the duties of the treasurer—

The Treasurer shall have such duties as may be assigned by the President or the Board of Directors from time to time and shall perform all duties incident to the office of Treasurer including but not limited to the following: (1) Having custody of and responsibility for all funds and securities belonging to the corporation. (2) Receiving and giving receipts for moneys paid to the corporation from whatever source and the deposit of the same, in the name of the corporation, in depositories duly authorized by the corporation. (3) Maintaining appropriate accounts and records for the corporation as required by law. (4) Having charge of the preparation of financial statements of the corporation according to Generally Accepted Accounting Principles.

The following is a "catch all" provision for the bylaws that allows the board of directors to create new offices without the need of amending the bylaws:

R-33.   Bylaw provision allowing for the appointment of additional officers as the board sees fit—

In addition to the offices established pursuant to these bylaws, the board of directors may create additional offices and appoint additional officers from time to time.

Appointment and Termination of Officers

Who Can Choose an Officer?

Officers are appointed by the board of directors, often but not necessarily upon the recommendation of current officers. (Note that directors are *elected* and officers are *appointed*.)

Below are two resolutions, the first appointing an officer, and the second appointing a whole slate of officers at once as frequently happens when a corporation is organized or acquired by new owners.

R-34.   Directors' resolution appointing a new officer—

RESOLVED, that **[name of officer]** is hereby appointed to the office of **[title]** of the corporation effective **[date appointment begins]** to hold such office until **[his/her]** death, resignation, retirement, removal, disqualification, or the appointment of a successor.

R-35.   Directors' resolution appointing a slate of officers—

RESOLVED, that the following individuals are hereby appointed to the offices indicated opposite their names, each of them to hold such office until his or her death, resignation, retirement, removal, disqualification, or the appointment of a successor:

[Name of officer]	[Office to which appointed]
[Name of officer]	[Office to which appointed]
[Name of officer]	[Office to which appointed]
[Etc.]	

The Officer as Employee

An officer is always an agent of the corporation, but it is not always true that an officer is an employee of the corporation. For example, an officer may be the employee of a parent corporation who serves as an officer of a subsidiary as a convenience to the employer parent. Or the corporation may be a small family company where a spouse serves as secretary or assistant secretary as a convenience to the person who runs the business.

Where the officer is an employee, it may be desirable to have a written employment contract. Form 39 is a simple employment agreement for a company officer. Space is provided to fill in the appropriate job description for each officer. (To add an indemnification provision, see Form 44 and pages 135 and 136.) Many employment agreements are, of course, much more elaborate. On the following page is an example of Form 39 completed for the office of president:

Employment agreement (president)—

Employment Agreement

This employment agreement is made by between __Raymond Rodriguez_____

_____ (the "Employee")

and _____Scrupulous Corporation_____

(the "Corporation"). It is agreed by the Employee and the Corporation as follows:

1. The Board of Directors of the corporation has duly appointed the Employee to the office of ____President_____ subject to the terms and conditions of this agreement.

2. Such appointment shall be effective on __January 1, 1997_____ at which time the Employee shall begin employment and assume the duties and authorities of ____President_____.

3. The duties of the _____President_____ shall be as follows:
To act as chief executive officer of the corporation and, subject to the direction and control of the Board of Directors, to supervise and manage the business affairs of the corporation, and to perform other duties as stated in the bylaws of the corporation. The President shall, when present, preside at meetings of the shareholders.

4. The Employee's salary and benefits during the term of this agreement shall be as stated in this paragraph, and may be adjusted from time to time by action of the Board of Directors of the Corporation.
$50,000 per year, plus group life insurance, and health insurance for the employee and his wife and minor children.

5. Employment pursuant to this agreement shall be:

☒ for a period of __3____ years beginning on the effective date stated above.

❑ at will and may be ended by the Employee or by action of the Board of Directors of the corporation at any time and for any reason.

This agreement was executed by the Employee and by the Corporation by authority of its Board of Directors on __December 18, 1996_____.

Corporation: Employee:

By: _Henry Hardy_____   _Raymond Rodriguez_____
    Henry Hardy, President   Raymond Rodriguez

The following is a directors' resolution authorizing the execution of the employment contract:

R-36.   Directors' resolution authorizing the an officer's employment agreement—

WHEREAS, the management of the corporation has presented to the board of directors a proposed employment contract between the corporation and **[name of officer]** as **[title]** of the corporation, which contract is incorporated into **[these minutes/this consent to action]** by reference (management storage file no. **[your corporation's file number]**) and has recommended the approval of such contract, it is, after due consideration

RESOLVED, that the employment contract between the corporation and **[name of officer]** as **[title]** of the corporation presented to the board of directors is hereby approved and ratified, and further

RESOLVED, that the appropriate officers of the corporation are hereby authorized and directed to execute such contract effective **[date]**.

It is not required that there be a written employment contract, but as a minimum there should be a resolution of the directors establishing a salary and any other conditions of employment that are pertinent. Below is an example of such a resolution. See chapter 8 for other director actions that may be useful.

R-37.   Directors' resolution establishing an officer's salary—

RESOLVED, that the corporation shall pay to **[name of officer]**, for services rendered as **[title]** of the corporation, an annual salary of $**[amount]** in equal monthly payments, such salary to be effective on **[date]**, and further

RESOLVED, that as **[title]**, **[name of officer]** shall be entitled to receive **[other employment benefits provided]** during the period of **[his/her]** employment by the corporation.

RESIGNATION AND TERMINATION
Officers serve at the pleasure of the board of directors. An employment agreement with an officer may be for a specific term, say, five years, but that doesn't mean that the corporation must keep an officer it doesn't want. If the corporation removes the officer, it's not necessarily the same as firing him or her. The former officer could continue as an employee or hold another office. But depending on the employment contract, the corporation could be liable for damages caused to the officer/employee as a result of such removal.

Similarly, an officer with a contract can resign at any time, but if the resignation violates the agreement, the officer could be liable for damages. An example of an officer's resignation follows. It should be addressed to the board of directors which appointed him or her.

Officer's resignation—

```
Date:    January 2, 1998

To: The Board of Directors of Scrupulous Corporation.

    I hereby resign the office of Vice President of the corpora-
tion effective January 27, 1998 at 5:00 P.M.

                              Sincerely,

                              Henry Hardy
                              _____
                              Henry Hardy
```

The board may formally accept the resignation by a resolution, such as the one below, which should remove any possibility that the employee could later revoke the resignation.

R-38.   Directors' acceptance of an officer's resignation—

```
    RESOLVED, that the resignation of [name of officer] as [title] of the
corporation, effective [date and time] is hereby accepted.
```

The removal of an officer, whatever its legal consequences in the context of an employment agreement, is also easily accomplished by a resolution such as:

> **R-39.** **Directors' resolution terminating an officer's appointment—**
>
> RESOLVED, that [name of officer] is hereby removed from the office of [title] of the corporation, effective [date and time].

INCUMBENCY As is the case with the board of directors (see Form 12), the secretary is occasionally asked to certify the names of persons currently holding corporate offices. Form 40 is such a Certificate of Officers. An example follows:

Secretary's certification of office holders—

Certification of Officers by the Secretary of

Scrupulous Corporation

I hereby certify that I am the Corporate Secretary of the Corporation, that the individuals listed below have been duly elected to the offices of the Corporation appearing opposite their names, and that they continue to hold such offices on the date of this certification:

President: Raymond Rodriguez   Vice President: Hugh Hardy

Secretary: Roberta Moore   Treasurer: Calvin Collier

Other: Other:

Signed and the seal of the corporation affixed on September 18, 1998 .

Roberta Moore
Roberta Moore
Corporate Secretary

EMPLOYEES AND AGENTS 8

EMPLOYEE OR INDEPENDENT CONTRACTOR?

The difference between an *employee* and an *independent contractor* is an important distinction. An employer owes significant legal duties to an employee that it may not owe to an independent contractor. Perhaps even more important, an employer owes duties to the government on account of an employee such as taxes, workers' compensation and the like. An employer may be liable to a third party for the negligence of an employee where it would not be liable for the negligence of an independent contractor.

It is not always easy to tell which is which. Just because you and someone you hire explicitly agree between yourselves at the time of the hire that it will be an independent contractor relationship, that doesn't mean a court or the IRS will agree with you if the issue comes up later.

There's a list of factors to be considered. A "yes" answer to all or most of the following questions will likely mean that the person hired is an independent contractor rather than an employee:

1. Does the person hired exercise independent control over the details of the work such as the methods used to complete the job?

2. Is the person hired in a business different from that of the person hiring? (For example, a plumber is hired by a lawyer.)

3. Does the person hired work as a specialist without supervision by the person hiring?

4. Does the person hired supply his or her own tools?

5. Is the person hired for only a short period of time rather than consistently over a relatively long period?

6. Does the job require a relatively high degree of skill?

7. Is the person paid "by the job" rather than "by the hour"?

EMPLOYEES

It is not necessary to have a written employment contract, although, contracts for employment that cannot be completed within a year may not be enforceable unless they are in writing. Some corporations have a policy against it and hire their employees *at will*, meaning that they can be fired or can quit at any time. But often the law limits the conditions under which even an at will employee can be fired.

INDEPENDENT CONTRACTORS

Contracts with independent contractors don't have to be in writing either, but it's often even more important that they are written than an employment agreement. For one thing, the writing is an opportunity to state clearly that you intend it to be an independent contractor arrangement. Also, since by definition you have relatively little control over the way an independent contractor does the work, the writing may be your last chance to influence important matters like exactly what the job is and when it must be completed.

MANAGING EMPLOYEES

COMPENSATION

The management of personnel is an art form this book won't help you with, but keeping track of compensation, especially for the higher-paid employees is one of the duties of the board of directors and, as always, their actions must be recorded somehow. The following are directors' resolutions giving a raise to a single employee, giving a bonus to a single employee, and setting salaries for a group of employees for the new year. These may be easily adapted for other employees and specific situations.

R-40.   Directors' resolution authorizing a raise—

RESOLVED, that effective **[date]** the annual salary of **[name and title of employee]** shall be increased from its present rate to $**[amount]** per year payable **[monthly/weekly/etc.]**.

R-41.   Directors' resolution authorizing a bonus—

RESOLVED, that on or before **[date]** the appropriate officer of the corporation is authorized and directed to pay to **[name and title]**, on behalf of the corporation, a bonus in the amount of $**[amount]** in addition to **[his/her]** regular salary.

R-42.   Directors' resolution authorizing a new salary schedule—

RESOLVED, that for the twelve month period beginning **[date]** the annual salaries of the individuals named below shall be the amounts stated opposite their names payable in the manner indicated and that such salaries shall remain in effect until changed or superseded by action of this board of directors:

[Name]   [Annual salary]   [Payment period (monthly, weekly, etc.)]
[Name]   [Annual salary]   [Payment period (monthly, weekly, etc.)]

INDEPENDENT CONTRACT CONSULTANTS

Consultants are a category of independent contractors. Frequently they are hired without any sort of written agreement, but it's hard to imagine a situation in which a written agreement is not better. Many consultants will have their own standard form agreements for you to sign.

ACCOUNTANTS   Accountants provide a variety of services, from bookkeeping and preparation of tax forms to the formal audit of a company's financial statements. Audits are expensive and, for most corporations, not necessary. An audit may be required by some regulatory agency or by contract with some institution. Be careful that you don't lightly sign an agreement with a lender or some other party that requires the production of *audited financial statements*. You may be getting into more than you bargained for. The example below is a directors' resolution authorizing the engagement of accountants to do the job.

R-43.   Directors' resolution hiring outside auditors—

WHEREAS, management has presented to the board of directors a proposed engagement letter between **[name of accounting firm]** and the corporation pursuant to which such firm will provide auditing services to the corporation for the year ended **[date fiscal year ended]** (such letter is located in management storage file number **[file number]**), and

WHEREAS, after discussion, the board of directors believes it to be in the best interests of the corporation to enter into such agreement, it is therefore

RESOLVED, that the proposed engagement letter for auditing services between the corporation and **[name of accounting firm]** is hereby approved and confirmed, and further

RESOLVED, that the corporation shall seek the ratification of such appointment by the shareholders of the corporation at its next annual meeting of shareholders, and further

RESOLVED, that the appropriate officers of the corporation are authorized and directed to confirm such agreement and to take such actions as are necessary to obtain such ratification by shareholders.

LAWYERS   Lawyers are predictably creative about the ways in which you can pay them. Usually contracts for legal services provide for payment by the hour or, where the client is a plaintiff in a law suit asking for money damages, on a contingent basis. A contingent fee is an arrangement in which the lawyer gets a share of the client's recovery, whatever that may be. The following is a resolution for the hiring of a lawyer:

R-44.   Directors' resolution hiring a lawyer—

WHEREAS, management has presented to the board of directors a proposed engagement letter between **[name of law firm]** and the corporation pursuant to which such firm will provide legal consultation to the corporation in connection with **[brief description of matters on which the lawyers will advise]** (such letter is located in management storage file number **[file number]**), and

WHEREAS, after discussion, the board of directors believes it to be in the best interests of the corporation to enter into such agreement, it is therefore

RESOLVED, that the proposed engagement letter for legal services between the corporation and **[name of law firm]** is hereby approved, ratified and confirmed.

EMPLOYEE BENEFITS

At some point, you may want to set up various benefit programs for employees. In setting up some of these benefit programs, tax ramifications to both the corporation and the recipient may be important considerations. Due to such tax and other possible complications, the corporation would be well advised to seek outside professional assistance in developing the details of the plan. Also, in order to adopt some of these benefit programs, the bylaws or articles of incorporation may need to be amended. You will need to read your corporation's articles of incorporation to determine whether these programs can be established by the board of directors, or may only be established by the

127

shareholders, by amendment to the bylaws, or by amendment to the articles of incorporation. The following are basic resolutions for various types of benefit plans:

R-45.   Resolution to establish health care plan—

RESOLVED, that the employee health care plan, a copy of which is attached to the minutes of this meeting, is hereby adopted and approved, and

RESOLVED, that the officers of the corporation are hereby authorized and directed to take such action as is necessary to implement said plan.

R-46.   Resolution to establish group life insurance program—

RESOLVED, that the officers of the corporation are hereby authorized and directed to contract with an insurance provider for a group life insurance program with the following basic provisions:

1. Life insurance shall be provided to all employees with **[number of years]** or more years of service with the corporation;
2. Each employee's life insurance policy shall be **[fill in either "in the amount of $_____," or some other criteria, such as "in an amount equal to two years salary," etc.]** .
3. The entire cost of the group life insurance program shall be paid by the corporation.

Note: You might also want to include such other provisions as may be advised by your insurance carrier, as well as an option for employees to obtain higher amounts of coverage at their own expense. You can also use the format of the other employee benefit program resolutions by simply referring to a more detailed plan to be attached to the minutes of the meeting.

R-47. **Resolution to establish retirement plan—**

RESOLVED, that the employee retirement plan, a copy of which is attached to the minutes of this meeting, is hereby adopted and approved, and

RESOLVED, that the officers of the corporation are hereby authorized and directed to take whatever action they deem necessary to implement said retirement plan, including but not limited to retaining legal counsel or other financial professionals to ensure that said retirement plan complies with any federal or state requirements for registration and to obtain any tax classification or benefits as may be directed in said retirement plan.

R-48. **Resolution to establish profit sharing plan—**

RESOLVED, that the profit sharing plan, a copy of which is attached to the minutes of this meeting, is hereby adopted and approved, subject to a favorable ruling from the Internal Revenue Service that such plan meets the requirement of the Internal Revenue Code, Sections 401(a) and 404.

RESOLVED, that the Secretary of the corporation is hereby authorized and directed to take any action necessary to implement said profit sharing plan, including but not limited to executing the trust agreement pursuant to said plan, and

RESOLVED, that the officers of the corporation are hereby authorized and directed to retain legal counsel to provide whatever services the officers deem necessary to secure a ruling from the Internal Revenue Service that said profit sharing plan is qualified under the Internal Revenue Code, Section 401(a) and 404, and to put the profit sharing plan into operation; and to provide the board of directors with an opinion as to legal compliance.

R-49.   **Resolution to establish stock option plan—**

RESOLVED, that the stock option plan, a copy of which is attached to the minutes of this meeting, is hereby adopted and approved, and

RESOLVED, that a total of [number of shares] shares of the common stock of this corporation, without par value, shall be set aside for sale pursuant to the terms of said stock option plan.

Note: In order to accomplish implementation of the stock option plan, it may also be necessary for the shareholders to make a resolution increasing the total number of shares of stock (see resolution R-17). This will probably require an amendment to the articles of incorporation.

R-50.   **Resolution to establish comprehensive benefit plan—**

RESOLVED, that the comprehensive employee benefit plan, a copy of which is attached to the minutes of this meeting, is hereby adopted and approved, and

RESOLVED, that the officers of the corporation are hereby authorized and directed to take whatever action they deem necessary to implement said comprehensive employee benefit plan , including but not limited to retaining legal counsel or other financial professionals to ensure that said comprehensive employee benefit plan complies with any federal or state requirements, and to obtain any tax classification or tax benefits as may be directed in said retirement plan.

Noncompetition and Nondisclosure Agreements

For certain key employees (including officers), you may want to have them sign agreements not to compete with your corporation if they should leave your employ, or not to disclose certain confidential information to your competitors. Form 49 is such a Noncompetition and Nondisclosure Agreement. You will find places to add in any information particular to your type of business in order to make the form better fit your circumstances.

Powers of Attorney

A *power of attorney* is a written authority for someone to act as your agent. The person who acts as your agent is called an "attorney in fact." (This is not the same as your agent for legal matters, who is called an *attorney at law*.) An attorney in fact is usually not an employee of the company. If you want the vice president to perform some task on behalf of the company, you can simply have the board of directors authorize the act in a resolution. You don't need a separate document such as the ones below. But you may want someone who isn't already an agent to undertake some duty. For example, remember that a director is not an agent of the company. If for some reason you want a director to undertake the job of negotiating or executing a contract, the corporation might make him or her its attorney in fact for the purpose.

A power of attorney can be for a particular duty and expire when that duty is done (Form 41), or it can authorize a wide range of activity and last for an indefinite period of time (Form 42). A power of attorney can usually be revoked at any time by the person giving it (Form 43). Examples of specific and general powers of attorney, and a revocation, follow:

Simple power of attorney for a particular purpose—

Limited Power of Attorney

_____ Scrupulous Corporation _____ (the "Corporation")
hereby grants to _____ James Bond _____ (the "Agent")
a limited power of attorney. As the Corporation's attorney in fact, the Agent shall have full power and authority to undertake and perform the following on behalf of the Corporation:

    Execute a contract and financing documents for the purchase and financing of a 1998 Chevrolet Astro delivery van.

    By accepting this grant, the Agent agrees to act in a fiduciary capacity consistent with the reasonable best interests of the corporation. This power of attorney may be revoked by the Corporation at any time; however, any person dealing with the Agent as attorney in fact may rely on this appointment until receipt of actual notice of termination.

    IN WITNESS WHEREOF, the undersigned corporation has executed this power of attorney under seal and by authority of its board of directors on __May 9, 1998__ .

By: _Raymond Rodriguez_
      Raymond Rodriguez,   President

Attest: _Roberta Moore_
      Roberta Moore,   Secretary

STATE OF
COUNTY OF

    I certify that __Roberta Moore__ personally appeared before me on __May 10, 1998__ and acknowledged that (s)he is Secretary of __Scrupulous Corporation__ and that by authority duly given and as the act of the corporation, the foregoing instrument was signed in its name by its President, sealed with its corporate seal and attested by him/her as its Secretary.

Penny Moneypenny
Penny Moneypenny
Notary Public
Notary's commission expires: August 30, 2000

    I hereby accept the foregoing appointment as attorney in fact on __May 10, 1998__ .

James Bond
James Bond,   Attorney in Fact

General power of attorney—

General Power of Attorney

_____Scrupulous Corporation_____ (the "Corporation")
hereby grants to _____James Bond_____ (the "Agent")
a general power of attorney. As the Corporation's attorney in fact, the Agent shall have full power and authority to undertake any and all acts which may be lawfully undertaken on behalf of the corporation including but not limited to the right to buy, sell, lease, mortgage, assign, rent or otherwise dispose of any real or personal property belonging to the Corporation; to execute, accept, undertake and perform contracts in the name of the Corporation; to deposit, endorse, or withdraw funds to or from any bank depository of the Corporation; to initiate, defend or settle legal actions on behalf of the Corporation; and to retain any accountant, attorney or other advisor deemed by the Agent to be necessary to protect the interests of the Corporation in relation to such powers.

By accepting this grant, the Agent agrees to act in a fiduciary capacity consistent with the reasonable best interests of the Corporation. This power of attorney may be revoked by the Corporation at any time; however, any person dealing with the Agent as attorney in fact may rely on this appointment until receipt of actual notice of termination.

IN WITNESS WHEREOF, the undersigned corporation has executed this power of attorney under seal and by authority of its board of directors as of the date stated above.

Scrupulous Corporation

By: _*Raymond Rodriguez*_____
Raymond Rodriguez,   President

Attest:

Roberta Moore
_____
Roberta Moore,   Secretary

STATE OF
COUNTY OF

I certify that _____Roberta Moore_____ personally appeared before me on _May 10, 1998_____ and acknowledged that (s)he is Secretary of _Scrupulous Corporation_____ and that by authority duly given and as the act of the corporation, the foregoing instrument was signed in its name by its President, sealed with its corporate seal and attested by him/her as its Secretary.

Penny Moneypenny
_____
Penny Moneypenny
Notary Public
Notary's commission expires: August 30, 2000

I hereby accept the foregoing appointment as attorney in fact on _May 10, 1998____.

James Bond
_____
James Bond,   Attorney in Fact

Cancellation of a power of attorney—

Revocation of Power of Attorney

The appointment of _____James Bond_____
as the attorney in fact of the undersigned Corporation (the "Corporation") made on
_____May 10, 1998_____ is hereby revoked and terminated by the Corporation effective on this date.

Signed and the corporate seal affixed on ___October 25, 1998___.

By: *Raymond Rodriguez*_____
　　　　Raymond Rodriguez,　President

Attest:

*Roberta Moore*_____
Roberta Moore,　　　Secretary

Protecting the Officers and Directors from Liability 9

Statutory Indemnification and Exculpation

There is a tension in the law between two strong public policy goals. On the one hand, we would like boards of directors to be populated by intelligent, experienced people who are willing to provide their judgment and expertise at low cost to the company. On the other hand, we would like the law to strictly scrutinize the activities of directors and severely punish those who, by being negligent or dishonest, wind up costing the company money. If we push the latter policy, we risk making the potential liability of directors too great and discouraging good people from serving. If we are too lenient, in the hope of making it easier for people to serve, we place corporations in danger from unscrupulous or incompetent directors. From time to time, the legal pendulum swings from one policy goal to the other.

There are several ways to protect directors and officers from liability. One is a rule of law called the *business judgment rule* that protects management from liability for damages resulting from a decision that turns out badly for the corporation. The rule protects management so long as the decision, even though a bad one, was made in good faith, on adequate information, and within management's authority.

Beyond the protection afforded by the business judgment rule, corporations may, and in some cases must, provide additional protection by indemnifying officers and directors for liability and expenses they incur in performing their duties. Generally it is possible to afford greater protection to directors than to officers. Corporations may be able to buy insurance to pay such indemnification.

Some states now allow the articles of incorporation to relieve directors from much potential liability by including an "exculpation" clause in the articles. Such clauses usually provide that, to the extent permitted by law, the directors will not be personally liable to the corporation or to the shareholders for monetary damages for breach of the director's duty to the corporation. Such a provision preserves the company's right to obtain an injunction from a court ordering the director to stop whatever he or she is doing that is in breach of the director's duty.

Indemnification of Officers and Directors

INDEMNIFICATION
BY CONTRACT

Form 44 is an agreement between a corporation and a director. On the following page is an example of such an agreement completed, followed by a provision for indemnification that might be included in an officer's employment contract. The intent is to require the corporation to indemnify the director or officer to the greatest extent allowed by law. A corporation should not lightly agree to such an arrangement, as it could subject the company to considerable expense at the hands of a director or officer who turns out to be less than the best.

Indemnification agreement with a director—

Indemnification Agreement

This indemnification agreement is entered into by and between _____, (the "Corporation") and
_____Scrupulous Corporation_____
_____Della Driskell_____, (the "Director").
In consideration of the Director's consent to serve or to continue serving as a director of the Corporation and other valuable consideration, the parties agree for themselves, their successors and assigns, as follows.

1.   Subject to the terms and limitations provided in this agreement, the Corporation hereby agrees to indemnify and hold the Director harmless to the fullest extent permitted by law against the expenses, payments and liabilities described in this agreement and incurred by the Director by reason of the fact that the Director is or was a director, officer, employee or agent of the Corporation or serves or served, at the request of the Corporation, as a director, officer, partner, trustee, employee, or agent of any other enterprise or as a trustee or administrator under an employee benefit plan.

1.1. The expenses, payments and liabilities referred to above are:

1.1.1.   Reasonable expenses, including attorneys' fees, incurred by the Director in connection with any threatened, pending, or completed inquiry, proceeding, action, suit, investigation or arbitration, whether civil, criminal, or administrative, and any appeal therefrom, whether or not brought by or on behalf of the Corporation.

1.1.2.   Any payment made by the Director in satisfaction of any judgment, money decree, fine, excise tax, penalty, or reasonable settlement for which the Director became liable in any matter described in subparagraph 1.1.1 above.

1.1.3.   Reasonable expenses, including legal fees, incurred by the Director in enforcing his or her rights under this paragraph.

1.2. To the fullest extent allowed by law, the Corporation shall pay the expenses and payments described in paragraph 1.1 above in advance of the final disposition of any matter.

2.   The rights of the Director hereunder shall inure to the benefit of the Director and his or her heirs, legal representative and assigns.

3.   The Director shall have the rights provided for in this agreement whether or not he or she is an officer, director, employee, or agent at the time such liabilities or expenses are imposed or incurred, and whether or not the claim asserted against the Director is based on matters that predate the execution of this agreement.

4.   The rights of the Director under this agreement are in addition to and not exclusive of any other rights to which he or she may be entitled under any statute, agreement, insurance policy, or otherwise.

5.   The Corporation agrees to use its best reasonable efforts to obtain and pay for a policy of insurance to protect and insure the Director's rights under this agreement.

IN WITNESS WHEREOF, the parties have executed this agreement under seal and by authority of its board of directors on _February 16, 1998_.

Corporation: Director:

By: *Raymond Rodriguez*   *Della Driskell*
     President

Attest: *Roberta Moore*_____, Secretary

Employment contract provision regarding indemnification of an officer—

Subject only to the terms and limitations provided in this paragraph, the Corporation hereby agrees to indemnify and hold Della Driskell harmless to the fullest extent permitted by law against the expenses, payments and liabilities described in this paragraph and incurred by Della Driskell by reason of the fact that Della Driskell is or was an officer, director, employee or agent of the Corporation or serves or served, at the request of the Corporation, as a director, officer, partner, trustee, employee, or agent of any other enterprise or as a trustee or administrator under an employee benefit plan.

1. The expenses, payments and liabilities referred to above are:

    1.1. Reasonable expenses, including attorneys' fees, incurred by Della Driskell in connection with any threatened, pending, or completed inquiry, proceeding, action, suit, investigation or arbitration, whether civil, criminal, or administrative, and any appeal therefrom, whether or not brought by or on behalf of the Corporation.

    1.2. Any payment made by Della Driskell in satisfaction of any judgment, money decree, fine, excise tax, penalty, or reasonable settlement for which Della Driskell became liable in any matter described in subparagraph 1.1 above.

    1.3. Reasonable expenses, including legal fees, incurred by Della Driskell in enforcing her rights under this paragraph.

2. To the fullest extent allowed by law, the Corporation shall pay the expenses and payments described in paragraph 1 above in advance of the final disposition of any matter.

3. The rights of Della Driskell under this paragraph shall inure to the benefit of Della Driskell and her heirs, legal representative and assigns.

4. Della Driskell shall have the rights provided for in this paragraph whether or not she is an officer, director, employee, or agent at the time such liabilities or expenses are imposed or incurred, and whether or not the claim asserted against Della Driskell is based on matters that predate the execution of this agreement.

5. The rights of Della Driskell under this provision are in addition to and not exclusive of any other rights to which she may be entitled under any statute, agreement, insurance policy, or otherwise.

6. The Corporation agrees to use its best reasonable efforts to obtain and pay for a policy of insurance to protect and insure Della Driskell's rights under this agreement.

INDEMNIFICATION
IN THE BYLAWS

The provision below takes a different approach. It is a provision to be included in the bylaws and grants indemnification rights to all directors. It is possible to include officers in such a scheme, but many corporations find it wiser to deal with the officers on a case by case basis, picking and choosing the ones to receive the benefits of such an arrangement. It is better to have a provision such as this adopted (or later approved or ratified) by the shareholders. If the directors adopt such a provision benefiting themselves, it is likely to be more open to challenge than if the shareholders had approved it.

R-51.   Bylaw provision requiring broad indemnification of officers and directors—

The Corporation shall indemnify and hold harmless to the fullest extent permitted by law any person who at any time serves or has served as a director of the corporation, and any such director who, at the request of the corporation, serves or served as a director, officer, partner, trustee, employee, or agent of any other enterprise or as a trustee or administrator under an employee benefit plan, against the expenses, payments and liabilities described in this paragraph below which were incurred by such person by reason of the fact that he or she served in any such capacities.

The expenses, payments and liabilities referred to above are: (1) reasonable expenses, including attorneys' fees, incurred by the Director in connection with any threatened, pending, or completed inquiry, proceeding, action, suit, investigation or arbitration, whether civil, criminal, or administrative, and any appeal therefrom, whether or not brought by or on behalf of the Corporation; (2) any payment made by the Director in satisfaction of any judgment, money decree, fine, excise tax, penalty, or reasonable settlement for which the Director became liable in any matter described in this paragraph above; and (3) reasonable expenses including legal fees incurred by the Director in enforcing his or her rights under this paragraph.

To the fullest extent allowed by law, the Corporation shall pay the expenses and payments allowed pursuant to this paragraph in advance of the final disposition of any matter. The rights of any Director hereunder shall inure to the benefit of the Director and his or her heirs, legal representative and assigns. A Director shall have the rights provided for in this paragraph whether or not he or she is a director at the time such liabilities or expenses are imposed or incurred, and whether or not the claim asserted against the Director is based on matters that predate the adoption of this bylaw provision. The rights of a Director hereunder are in addition to and not exclusive of any other rights to which he or she may be entitled under any statute, agreement, insurance policy, or otherwise. Any person who at any time after adoption of this bylaw serves or has served in a capacity so as to allow him or her indemnification hereunder shall be deemed to have done so in reliance upon, and as consideration for, the indemnification rights provided in this bylaw.

> The Board of Directors of the corporation shall take all such action and make all such determinations as may be necessary or desirable under the law to properly authorize the payment of the indemnification provided by this bylaw, including, without limitation, establishing special committees of the board of directors, hiring special counsel and/or obtaining shareholder approval of such indemnification.
>
> The Corporation shall obtain a policy of insurance to protect and insure the Directors' rights under this agreement.

INSURANCE

The indemnification schemes discussed above are of use only if the corporation has funds to pay the indemnification when it is due. It is the nature of things that law suits against directors and officers are rare when times are good and all too frequent when the corporation is in trouble. A corporation in so much trouble that the directors are being sued by the shareholders may not have money to pay indemnification. Insurance policies to protect directors and officers in case they are sued for a breach of their duties to the corporation, called *errors and omissions* coverage, can fill that gap, but they also can be difficult to get, and where available, impossibly expensive for many corporations. Below is an example of a resolution for purchasing such insurance:

> **R-52.** Directors' resolution approving the purchase of indemnification coverage for officers and directors—
>
> WHEREAS, the management of the corporation has presented to the board of directors a proposed policy of insurance negotiated with **[name of insurer]** and titled **[title of policy]** providing errors and omissions coverage for the officers and directors of the corporation and insuring the company's obligations to pay indemnification to its officers and directors pursuant to the bylaws of the company and various contractual arrangements, which policy is incorporated into **[these minutes/this consent to action]** by reference (management storage file no. **[file number]**) and

WHEREAS, management has recommended the approval of the purchase of such policy, it is, after due consideration

RESOLVED, that the policy of insurance negotiated with **[name of insurer]** and titled **[title of policy]** presented to the board of directors is hereby approved and ratified, and further

RESOLVED, that the appropriate officers are authorized and directed to take such actions and execute such documents as are necessary or desirable to place such policy in effect and make and to continue to make premium payments from corporate funds necessary to keep such policy in force until further action by this board.

CONFLICTS OF INTEREST

When can the corporation enter into a contract with one of its officers or directors? Corporations often enter into contracts with individual officers or directors. For example a small company may want to borrow money from a director, or buy real estate, or lease office space. Where such arrangements have been proven unfair to the corporation, courts have set them aside and relieved the corporation of any obligation to perform under the agreements, or have allowed the corporation to recover damages from the director or officer who allegedly took advantage of the company over which he or she had influence. The MBCA (Sec. 8.31) makes it clear that a contract between the corporation and one of its officers or directors is enforceable so long as the facts of the conflict are known to the board of directors, which, nevertheless, approves the contract; or the facts are known to the shareholders and they approve it; or the contract is fair to the corporation in any case.

What can be done to avoid or minimize conflicts of interest? Here is where properly recorded minutes of a directors meeting can be very valuable. The following example of minutes records the action of directors in approving a contract between one of the directors and the company.

Minutes of directors meeting authorizing the purchase of property from a director—

Mr. Rodriguez next reported on the company's need for additional office space, explaining that the number of employees has expanded greatly since its present location was first occupied. Mr. Rodriguez explained that the report he was about to present involved a potential conflict of interest between the corporation and Mr. Henry Hardy, one of the company's directors.

Mr. Hardy stated that he was aware of the potential conflict and that he wished therefore to avoid taking part in any discussion of the matter. He asked that he be excused from the meeting and assured the directors that he would be available to answer any questions that might arise during the board's deliberations.

After Mr. Hardy left the meeting, the President's report was distributed to the remaining directors. A copy of the report is filed in management storage file No. 94-56. The directors noted that figures presented by Mr. Rodriguez in his report predicted that the company would gain substantial savings over a five year period by purchasing and expanding onto the vacant lot adjacent to the company's present location compared to the renting of additional needed space or relocation of the company's operation elsewhere.

Such property, it was noted, belonged to Mr. Henry Hardy. Mr. Rodriguez reported that the property had belonged to the Hardy family for many years. Mr. Rodriguez reported that, while Mr. Hardy was reluctant to sell the property, the company, through its general counsel had succeeded in negotiating its purchase for $145,000 under the terms of a proposed contract included in the President's report. The property had been appraised by an independent professional appraiser whose report was also included in the President's report and showed the proposed purchase price to be within the range of values reported by the appraiser.

The Board then reviewed the appraisal report and the proposed purchase contract in detail. After discussion, the following resolutions, moved for adoption by Ms. Driskell, seconded by Ms. Moore, were adopted.

RESOLVED, that the proposed contract for the purchase of the lot adjacent to the company's headquarters as described in the President's report presented to this meeting (management storage file No. 94-56) for a cash purchase price of $145,000 is hereby approved and ratified, and further

RESOLVED, that the board of directors, noting that such property belongs to Mr. Hugh Hardy, a member of the board of directors and shareholder of the company, specifically finds that the proposed contract and purchase price is reasonable and fair to the corporation, and further

RESOLVED, that the officers of the corporation are authorized to execute such contract together with such other documents as may be necessary or desirable to complete the described purchase within 120 days of the date of this resolution.

AMENDING BYLAWS AND ARTICLES OF INCORPORATION

10

AMENDING BYLAWS

One advantages of company bylaws is that they are easy to amend compared to the articles of incorporation. In almost all cases, the shareholders must vote to change the articles, and a filing must be made at the office of the secretary of state or other appropriate agency. In most cases, when you want to make a change in the bylaws, it will be the directors who do it. But the shareholders also have the power to do so.

AMENDMENT BY SHAREHOLDERS

When should the shareholders amend the bylaws? For most corporations (depending on the way your articles and bylaws read—there will be a section in the bylaws on amendments) the rule is that the shareholders can amend the bylaws by majority vote any way they want to consistent with state law. However, once the shareholders have adopted or amended a provision of the bylaws, they may limit the power of the directors to change it later. As a practical matter, you don't want the shareholders to amend the bylaws except to enact a provision that the shareholders don't want the directors to be able to change without shareholder permission. Provisions specifying important rights having to do with the shareholders are the most common examples, for instance, limitations on the rights of shareholders to dispose of their shares. There are special statutory rules about amending quorum and voting requirements for shareholders and directors (MBCA, Sec. 10.21 and Sec. 10.22).

AMENDMENT BY
DIRECTORS

When should the directors amend the bylaws? In most cases, if the bylaws need amending, it is the directors who should do it. Of course, it follows from the previous paragraph, that if the provision to be amended is one that was adopted or previously amended by the shareholders, it may be that the directors cannot do it. And if it is a provision that the shareholders don't want the directors to be able to change later, then the directors should not do it.

Below is a resolution for adoption by either the directors or the shareholders to amend the bylaws. In this and other forms contained in this book, where a document is amended, the amended provision is to be restated in full in the resolution. It is not absolutely necessary to do so, but does reduce the possibility that someone will misread the amendment in the context of the provision, thus defeating the intent of the amendment. Also below, is a resolution which amends the bylaws by adding an entirely new paragraph.

R-53. **Resolution amending bylaws of the corporation by changing an existing provision—**

RESOLVED, that, pursuant to **[article and section number of the bylaws authorizing amendments]** of the bylaws of the corporation, **[article and section number of the bylaws to be amended]** of such bylaws is hereby amended to read in its entirety as follows:

[insert the paragraph of the bylaws as amended]

R-54. **Resolution amending the bylaws of the corporation by adding a new provision—**

RESOLVED, that, pursuant to **[article and section number of the bylaws authorizing amendments]** of the bylaws of the corporation, such bylaws are hereby amended by the addition of a new provision at **[article and section number of the new provision]** to read in its entirety as follows:

[insert the new paragraph]

AMENDING ARTICLES OF INCORPORATION

STATUTORY
REQUIREMENTS

Most state statutes allow some simple changes in the articles of incorporation to be made by the directors acting alone (MBCA, Sec. 10.02 and Sec. 10.05), but in most cases it takes both directors and shareholders to amend the articles. The directors recommend the change to the shareholders, and the shareholders either approve or disapprove the proposed change. Under the statute, the only occasion on which a proposed amendment may be presented to the shareholders without the directors' positive recommendation is when the directors have a conflict of interest, or when some other special circumstance makes it inappropriate to make a recommendation. In that case, the directors must explain why there is no recommendation.

If there is to be a shareholders meeting (remember the vote can be made by unanimous written consent), the company must give notice to the shareholders stating the purpose of the meeting and enclosing a copy of the proposed amendment (MBCA, Sec. 10.03).

After the amendment has been adopted by the shareholders, "articles of amendment" must be filed with the state (MBCA, Sec. 10.08).

DISSENTERS'
RIGHTS

Some changes in a corporation so seriously affect the existing rights of shareholders that shareholders who *dissent from* (vote against) the action are allowed to opt out and have their shares purchased by the corporation at *fair market value* (MBCA, Chapter 13). Many of these actions arise in the context of amending the articles of incorporation. Dissenters' rights is a complicated issue beyond the scope of this book, and failure to follow the statutory procedures exactly may undo any amendment you attempt, in addition to creating substantial liability. For that reason you should consult your attorney before attempting to do more than the most innocuous of amendments to the articles. A corporation with more than one class of shareholders may also encounter special difficulties in amending its articles, in which case a lawyer's advice would be particularly useful.

The following is a directors' resolution recommending an amendment to the articles of incorporation to the shareholders. Next, is a shareholders' resolution approving the amendment. Your state may have a fill-in-the-blank form which must be used for the amendment of articles of incorporation.If not, you can use Form 51. An example of Form 51 completed may be found in chapter 11. The amendment usually becomes effective when the articles of amendment are filed.

R-55. **Directors' resolution recommending an amendment to the articles of incorporation—**

RESOLVED, that pursuant to the laws of the state of [state of incorporation] and the articles and bylaws of the corporation, the board of directors hereby recommends to the shareholders of the corporation that its articles of incorporation be amended by changing [article to be amended] to read in its entirety as follows:

[insert the article as amended]

FURTHER RESOLVED, that the submission of such proposed amendment to the shareholders for approval shall be on the condition that the directors, by majority vote, may withdraw and cancel the amendment at any time prior to its effective date,

FURTHER RESOLVED, that the appropriate officers of the corporation are hereby authorized and directed to call a special meeting of the shareholders, giving appropriate notice, on [date or range of dates for the meeting] for the purpose of approving or disapproving such proposed amendment, and, upon approval by the shareholders, to execute and file articles of amendment and to take such other actions as may be necessary or desirable to give effect to the proposed amendment and the foregoing resolutions.

R-56. **Shareholders' resolution adopting the recommended amendment—**

WHEREAS the directors of the corporation have proposed that its articles of incorporation be amended in the manner set out below, and recommended to the shareholders that such amendment be adopted by its shareholders, it is therefore

RESOLVED, that such proposal and recommendation by the directors is hereby ratified and approved and that the articles of incorporation of the corporation are hereby amended by changing [article to be amended] to read in its entirety as follows:

[insert the article as amended]

CHANGING THE CORPORATE NAME 11

CAN WE USE THE NAME WE WANT?

Many people incorrectly believe that, because a corporation has incorporated under a certain name, that name cannot be used by any other business. When your corporation was created, it is very likely your lawyer asked you to suggest several possible names for it. The lawyer then checked with the state to see if the names you liked were available, that is, whether there were any already existing corporations with the same or very similar names. However, for a name to be available for use, it is sufficient that it differs only slightly from existing names—maybe only a spelling difference. Even so, the fact that a name has been used by a corporation does not mean that the same name couldn't be adopted by a partnership or sole proprietorship or by a corporation in another state.

Just because a name is "available" according to the standards of your secretary of state, it doesn't mean you may legally use it. It may be that the name is the registered trademark or service mark of another company and that your use of the name would violate the rights of the mark's owner. Only a trademark search will discover whether this is true.

ADOPTING A CORPORATE ALIAS

One way to change the name of your business is to adopt an assumed or fictitious name. This method is simple and quick. Usually, it does not require that you check with the state to see if a name is available. However, if you adopt as an alias a name that is someone else's trademark, you may be liable for infringement. So that people dealing with your company have fair notice of your company's true identity, the states require that you file a formal declaration of the alias. These filing requirements vary quite a bit from state to state. Sometimes the filing must be done with a state agency, sometimes with the city or county where the corporation conducts its business, and sometimes both. A company could have several different assumed names. For example it may conduct a fast food business under one name and sell television sets at a different location under another. Below is a directors' resolution authorizing the use of an assumed name, followed by an example of a typical formal declaration that lets the public know who they are dealing with. This form may vary substantially from the one required in your state. The statute dealing with the filing requirement may well be located somewhere other than in your state's corporations act since partnerships and sole proprietorships which adopt aliases are also required to make such a filing.

R-57.   **Directors' resolution authorizing the adoption of an assumed name—**

RESOLVED, that the corporation shall assume and henceforth conduct its **[Optional: describe a particular business operation]** business under the name **[Name to be used]**, and

FURTHER RESOLVED, that the appropriate officers of the corporation are hereby authorized and directed to execute and file such certificates and declarations as may be required by law and to take such other acts as may be necessary or desirable to give effect to the foregoing resolution.

Certificate of Assumed Name—

Assumed Name Certificate

The undersigned corporation, which intends to engage in business in Jamaica County, New York, under an assumed name, hereby certifies that:

1. The name under which the business is to be conducted is: _____
_____ Home Safety Systems _____.

2. The nature of the business to be conducted under the assumed name is: _____ manufacture and sale of home security equipment _____.

3. The name and address of the owner of such business is: _____
____ Scrupulous Corporation, P.O. Box 19, New York, NY 10032 ____.

IN WITNESS WHEREOF, the corporation has caused this certificate to be executed under seal and by authority of its board of director as of __ March 26, 1998 __.

Scrupulous Corporation

By: *Raymond Rodriguez* _____
Raymond Rodriguez, President

Attest:
Roberta Moore _____
Roberta Moore, Secretary

CHANGING THE CORPORATION'S NAME IN THE ARTICLES OF INCORPORATION

AMENDING THE ARTICLES OF INCORPORATION

It is in the articles of incorporation that a corporation's name is officially adopted. In order to change the official name, therefore, the articles of incorporation must be amended. (See the discussion of the procedure for amending articles of incorporation in chapter 10.) On the following page is a directors resolution to recommend a name change, and a shareholders resolution adopting the name change.

R-58.   Directors' resolution recommending the name change to the shareholders—

RESOLVED, that pursuant to the laws of the state of **[state of incorporation]** and the articles and bylaws of the corporation, the board of directors hereby recommends to the shareholders of the corporation that its articles of incorporation be amended to change the name of the corporation from its current name to **[new name]**, and

FURTHER RESOLVED, that such change be accomplished by amending **[article to be amended]** to read in its entirety as follows:

ARTICLE **[article number]**. The name of the corporation is **[new name]**.

FURTHER RESOLVED, that the submission of such proposed amendment to the shareholders for approval shall be on the condition that the directors, by majority vote, may withdraw and cancel the amendment at any time prior to its effective date,

FURTHER RESOLVED, that the appropriate officers of the corporation are hereby authorized and directed to call a special meeting of the shareholders, giving appropriate notice, on **[date or range of dates for the meeting]** for the purpose of approving or disapproving such proposed amendment, and, upon approval by the shareholders, to execute and file articles of amendment and to take such other actions as may be necessary or desirable to give effect to the proposed amendment and the foregoing resolutions.

R-59.   Shareholders' resolution adopting the change—

WHEREAS the directors of the corporation have proposed that its articles of incorporation be amended so as to change the name of the corporation, and recommended to the shareholders that such amendment be adopted by its shareholders, it is therefore

RESOLVED, that such proposal and recommendation by the directors is hereby ratified and approved and that the articles of incorporation of the corporation are hereby amended by changing **[article to be amended]** to read in its entirety as follows:

ARTICLE **[article number]**. The name of the corporation is **[new name]**.

Articles of Amendment changing the name of the corporation—

Articles of Amendment of

Scrupulous Corporation

The Articles of Incorporation of ___Scrupulous Corporation___ are hereby amended as follows:

1.   The name of the corporation is ___Scrupulous Corporation___.

2.   The following amendment to the company's articles of incorporation was adopted by its shareholders on ___December 14___, ___1998___ as prescribed by law:

The articles of incorporation of the corporation are hereby amended by changing Article ___6___ to read in its entirety as follows:

ARTICLE ___6___. The name of the corporation is ___Scrupulous America, Inc.___

3.   At the time of such adoption, the number of shares of the corporation outstanding was ___100,000___; and the number of votes entitled to be voted on the adoption was ___100,000___; and the number of votes indisputably represented at the meeting of shareholders was ___100,000___ shares at the meeting in person and by proxy whose voting rights were uncontested.

4.   The number of undisputed votes cast for the amendment was ___100,000___, a number sufficient for adoption of the proposed amendment.

5.   These articles will become effective at the date and time of their filing.

The date of these Articles of Amendment is ___December 28, 1998___.

Scrupulous Corporation

By: ___*Raymond Rodriguez*___
Raymond Rodriguez, President

NAME CHANGES
AND STOCK
CERTIFICATES

After a name change, what is done about the old share certificates? After the corporation has a new name, it will still have stock certificates circulating bearing the old name. There is no harm in this, and frequently the corporation will allow the old certificates to remain outstanding. When shares are traded, the new shareholder may ask to have new certificates issued bearing the new name.

The company may want to call in the old certificates and issue new ones in their place. It's difficult to force shareholders to cooperate in this effort, but it helps to make the process as simple as possible. The following is a letter requesting such cooperation from a shareholder.

Letter to shareholders requesting the exchange of old certificates—

Scrupulous America, Inc.

400 West 61st Avenue, P.O. Box 19, New York, NY 10032

January 4, 1999

Henry Hardy
1440 Enterprise Blvd.
New York, NY 10033

Re: Share certificate(s) number(s): 000005

Dear Mr. Hardy:

Recently the shareholders of Scrupulous Corporation voted to change the company's name to Scrupulous America, Inc. The name change is now official, and your corporation would like to exchange your share certificate(s) for new certificates bearing the company's new name.

Enclosed for your convenience is an envelope addressed to the corporate secretary. Please place your certificates in the envelope and return them to the company. No postage is required. The Secretary will issue new share certificates in the same name or names as the old ones and send them to you by return mail to the address listed above. If you would like the certificates sent to a different address, please so indicate by changing the above address as appropriate and returning this letter to us along with your old shares.

Thank you for your cooperation.

Scrupulous America, Inc.

By: *Calvin Collier*
Calvin Collier, Treasurer

Mergers 12

What Is a Merger?

There are many different ways one business can acquire another. One company could buy the shares of another, after which the acquired company would be a subsidiary of the acquiring company. One company could buy the business assets of another, leaving behind a shell corporation that continues to be owned by its old shareholders. Or there could be a merger in which the acquired corporation becomes a part of and disappears into the acquiring corporation.

Each acquisition method has advantages and disadvantages. Depending on the type of business and the separate (often conflicting) concerns of the acquiring entity and the acquisition target and their various owners, some method or combination should be chosen that best serves the interests of the parties. The successful negotiation of an acquisition is not an easy task. Too often business people begin the process with insufficient experience or advice and reach an advanced stage in the process of agreement, only to find that they have overlooked some wrinkle in tax law, securities law or corporate law that frustrates the deal or greatly devalues it. Get the professional advice you need early enough to make it effective.

STATUTORY
METHODS FOR
MERGING
CORPORATIONS

Mergers between two, or among more than two, corporations can occur, because there are statutes that allow it to happen. In order for a merger to occur, the steps laid out in the statute must be followed carefully and completely or else the merger may be completely ineffective. It can be a complex procedure and shouldn't be attempted without competent legal advice.

There are many different kinds of mergers, differing chiefly in the number and relationships of the companies involved and the payment for shares given up by the shareholders whose company disappears into another company. For example, in a cash merger the shareholders of the acquired (non-surviving) corporation receive cash in exchange for their shares. Often the shareholders of the acquired corporation receive shares of the acquiring (surviving) corporation in exchange for their shares. In a *triangular merger* the acquired corporation disappears into a subsidiary which survives and its shareholders receive shares of the surviving subsidiary's parent. In a *reverse triangular merger* the acquired corporation survives as a subsidiary of the parent and its former shareholders receive shares of the parent in exchange for the shares of the acquired company. One form is frequently chosen over another for its tax consequences.

CORPORATIONS
OF DIFFERENT
STATES

What if the corporations are organized in different states? A corporation organized under the laws of one state may merge with a corporation organized under the laws of another state. In that case, the laws and procedures of both states must be followed exactly. Sometimes this leads to curious and annoying contradictions. For example the merger may become *effective* in one state before it does in the other. Each state may require similar but slightly different forms to be filed. If the surviving corporation wishes to continue conducting business in the state where the non-surviving corporation conducted its business, it will be necessary for the surviving corporation to *domesticate* in that state by filing additional forms which, among other things, designate a person in that state to be the agent on whom notice of law suits and other forms of process may be served.

UNAVOIDABLE
COMPLEXITIES
Some unavoidable complexities and what to do about them. Mergers and other forms of acquisition can have very serious tax effects and should not be undertaken without ample expert advice. If one or the other of the corporations involved has a substantial number of shareholders, the same securities regulations discussed in chapter 4 will apply. (In a merger, the shares of one or both of the corporations involved are bought and sold.) A vote of the shareholders may be required, in which case the securities regulations mentioned in chapter 5 will apply. The advice of an experienced securities lawyer may be indispensable.

MERGER OF A SUBSIDIARY CORPORATION INTO ITS PARENT

The usual procedure for a merger is similar to the procedure for amending the articles of incorporation. That is, the directors propose and recommend the merger and the shareholders then either approve or disapprove it. Also, as in the case of some amendments, some mergers may be accomplished by a short cut.

Where the merger is between a parent corporation and a wholly owned subsidiary (i.e., the parent owns 100% of the shares), the directors can do it alone without shareholder approval (MBCA, Sec. 11.04). That makes sense, because the shareholders own the same thing after the merger that they owned before—it's just arranged in a different set of boxes. (It's also possible even if up to ten percent of the shares of the subsidiary are owned by someone else, but the minority shareholders may be entitled to *dissenters' rights*, greatly complicating things. See chapter 10.) Provided the laws of both states allow it, you can accomplish a short form merger of this type between two corporations incorporated under the laws of different states.

In a merger, the directors of the parent corporation adopt a plan of merger and file articles of merger with the state incorporating the plan (Form 45 or Form 46) .

R-60.   **Directors' resolution adopting a plan of merger—**

RESOLVED, that the following plan of merger between this corporation and its wholly owned subsidiary, **[name of subsidiary]**, is hereby approved and adopted:

Plan of Merger

A. The name of the parent corporation into which the subsidiary shall merge is **[name of parent]**, which shall be the Surviving Corporation, and the name of the subsidiary corporation which shall merge into the parent is **[name of subsidiary]**, which shall be the Merging Corporation.

B. On the effective date of the merger, the Merging Corporation shall merge into the Surviving Corporation and the corporate existence of the Merging Corporation shall cease. The shares of the Merging Corporation shall not be converted into shares, obligations or other securities of the Surviving Corporation or any other corporation or into cash or other property in whole or in part. The outstanding shares of the Surviving Corporation will not be converted, exchanged or altered in any manner, but shall remain outstanding shares of the Surviving Corporation.

C. The directors of the Surviving Corporation may, in their discretion, abandon this merger at any time before its effective date.

D. The effective date of this merger shall be the close of business on the date articles of merger relating to this merger are filed as required by law.

FURTHER RESOLVED, that the corporation as shareholder of the Merging Corporation hereby waives all notice of the proposed merger, and

FURTHER RESOLVED, that the appropriate officers of the corporation are hereby authorized and directed to execute and file articles of merger and to take such other actions as may be necessary or desirable to give effect to the foregoing resolution.

Articles of Merger (short form)—

Articles of Merger of

Honor Corporation

into

Scrupulous Corporation

These Articles of Merger are submitted by <u>Scrupulous Corporation</u>, organized under the laws of <u>Nevada</u> (the "Surviving Corporation") for the purpose of merging its subsidiary corporation <u>Honor Corporation</u>, organized under the laws of <u>New York</u> (the "Merging Corporation") into the Surviving Corporation.

1. The following Plan of Merger has been duly approved by the board of directors of the surviving corporation

Plan of Merger

A. The name of the parent corporation into which the subsidiary shall merge is <u>Scrupulous Corporation</u>, which shall be the Surviving Corporation, and the name of the subsidiary corporation which shall merge into the parent is <u>Honor Corporation</u>, which shall be the Merging Corporation.

B. On the effective date of the merger, the Merging Corporation shall merge into the Surviving Corporation and the corporate existence of the Merging Corporation shall cease. The shares of the Merging Corporation shall not be converted into shares, obligations or other securities of the Surviving Corporation or any other corporation or into cash or other property in whole or in part. The outstanding shares of the Surviving Corporation will not be converted, exchanged or altered in any manner, but shall remain outstanding shares of the Surviving Corporation.

C. The directors of the Surviving Corporation may, in their discretion, abandon this merger at any time before its effective date.

D. The effective date of this merger shall be the close of business on the date articles of merger relating to this merger are filed as required by law.

2. Shareholder approval of the merger was not required because the Surviving Corporation was the owner of 100% of the outstanding shares of the Merging Corporation, and the Plan of Merger does not provide for any amendment to the articles of incorporation of the Surviving Corporation.

These articles of merger were signed by the corporation on <u>April 1, 1999</u>.

Scrupulous Corporation

By: *Raymond Rodriguez*

Raymond Rodriguez, President

Merger of Corporations With Different Owners

Board of Directors and Shareholders

As you would expect, when the corporations intending to merge have different owners, the owners must have a chance to approve or disapprove the proposal. In a merger of independent corporations, the shareholders are acquiring and disposing of property, not just rearranging it. So the directors of the corporations must recommend the proposed merger to the shareholders, and then the shareholders of each corporation must approve the proposed plan of merger. If the directors, because of a conflict of interest or for some other sufficient reason, believe they should not favorably recommend the proposed merger, they must explain to the shareholders why they can't take a position.

The complexities mentioned above must be carefully considered in the merger of two or more corporations with different owners, and the plan of merger will very likely be a much more complex document than the one in the previous example. In fact, where the corporations are any more than shell corporations, there will likely be a separate merger agreement that covers the many details inherent in combining two unique and ongoing business operations.

The three forms on the following two pages illustrate the kind of basic documents that would accomplish such a merger [i.e., a directors' resolution recommending a merger plan, a shareholders' resolution adopting the plan, and the "long form" Articles of Merger (Form 46)]. In the examples, one share of the surviving corporation will be issued for each share of the merging corporation; and after the merger is complete, the shareholders of the merging corporation will be new shareholders of the surviving corporation. An infinite number of other arrangements are possible, including some other ratio for issuing shares (e.g., two shares of the survivor for each share of the merging corporation) or cash given exchange for shares of the merging corporation.

R-61. Directors' resolution recommending a plan of merger to the shareholders—

RESOLVED, that pursuant to the laws of the state of [state of incorporation] and the articles and bylaws of the corporation, the board of directors hereby recommends to the shareholders of the corporation that the following Plan of Merger be adopted by the shareholders:

<u>Plan of Merger</u>

A. [Name of merging corporation], which shall be the Merging Corporation, shall merge into [name of surviving corporation], which shall be the Surviving Corporation.

B. On the effective date of the merger, the Merging Corporation shall merge into the Surviving Corporation and the corporate existence of the Merging Corporation shall cease. On the effective date of the merger, each outstanding share of the Merging Corporation shall be converted into one share of the Surviving Corporation. The outstanding shares of the Surviving Corporation will not be converted, exchanged or altered in any manner, but shall remain outstanding shares of the Surviving Corporation.

C. Each shareholder of the Merging Corporation holding a certificate representing share(s) of such corporation shall surrender such certificate and shall be entitled to receive certificate(s) representing the shares of the Surviving Corporation to which the Shareholder is entitled under this Plan of Merger. After the effective date of the merger and before such surrender, each certificate representing shares of the Merging Corporation shall be deemed for all purposes to evidence ownership of a like number of shares of the Surviving Corporation.

D. The directors of the Surviving Corporation or the Merging Corporation may, in their discretion abandon this merger at any time before its effective date.

E. The effective date of this merger shall be the close of business on the date articles of merger relating to this Plan of Merger are filed as required by law.

FURTHER RESOLVED, that the submission of such proposed Plan of Merger to the shareholders for approval shall be on the condition that the directors, by majority vote, may withdraw and cancel such proposed merger at any time prior to its effective date, and

FURTHER RESOLVED, that the appropriate officers of the corporation are hereby authorized and directed to call a special meeting of the shareholders, giving appropriate notice, on [date or range of dates for the meeting] for the purpose of approving or disapproving such Plan of Merger, and, upon approval by the shareholders of the corporations participating in the proposed merger, to execute and file articles of merger and to take such other actions as may be necessary or desirable to give effect to the Plan of Merger and the foregoing resolutions.

R-62.   Shareholders' resolution adopting a plan of merger—

WHEREAS the directors of the corporation have proposed the adoption of a Plan of Merger accomplishing the merger of **[Merging Corporation]** into **[Surviving Corporation]**, and have recommended to the shareholders that such Plan of Merger be adopted, it is therefore

RESOLVED, that such proposal and recommendation by the directors is hereby ratified and approved and that the following Plan of Merger is hereby adopted:

[insert Plan of Merger]

Articles of Merger (long form)—

Articles of Merger of
_____Home Safety Systems, Inc._____

into

_____Scrupulous Corporation_____

These   Articles   of   Merger   are   submitted   by
_____Scrupulous Corporation_____, organized under the laws of _____ (the "Surviving Corporation") for the purpose of merging ____Home Safety Systems, Inc.____, organized under the laws of _____New York_____ (the "Merging Corporation") into the Surviving Corporation.

1. The following Plan of Merger has been duly approved by the boards of directors of the Surviving Corporation and the Merging Corporation:

Plan of Merger

A. Home Safety Systems, Inc., which shall be the Merging Corporation, shall merge into Scrupulous Corporation, which shall be the Surviving Corporation.
B. On the effective date of the merger, the Merging

Corporation shall merge into the Surviving Corporation and the corporate existence of the Merging Corporation shall cease. On the effective date of the merger, each outstanding share of the Merging Corporation shall be converted into one share of the Surviving Corporation. The outstanding shares of the Surviving Corporation will not be converted, exchanged or altered in any manner, but shall remain outstanding shares of the Surviving Corporation.

C. Each shareholder of the Merging Corporation holding a certificate representing share(s) of such corporation shall surrender such certificate and shall be entitled to receive certificate(s) representing the shares of the Surviving Corporation to which the Shareholder is entitled under this Plan of Merger. After the effective date of the merger and before such surrender, each certificate representing shares of the Merging Corporation shall be deemed for all purposes to evidence ownership of a like number of shares of the Surviving Corporation.

D. The directors of the Surviving Corporation or the Merging Corporation may, in their discretion abandon this merger at any time before its effective date.

E. The effective date of this merger shall be the close of business on the date articles of merger relating to this Plan of Merger are filed as required by law.

2. The designation and number of outstanding shares, and the number of votes entitled to be cast by each voting group entitled to vote separately on such Plan as to the Merging Corporation were:

Designation:	Shares outstanding:	Votes entitled to be cast:
Common shares	1,000,000	1,000,000

The number of votes cast for such Plan by shareholders of the Merging Corporation was 890,000 which was sufficient for approval of the Plan by the shareholders of the Merging Corporation.

3. The designation and number of outstanding shares, and the number of votes entitled to be cast by each voting group entitled to vote separately on such Plan as to the Surviving Corporation were:

Designation:	Shares outstanding:	Votes entitled to be cast:
Common shares	100,000	100,000

The number of votes cast for such Plan by shareholders of the Surviving Corporation was ____100,000____ which was sufficient for approval of the Plan by the shareholders of the Surviving Corporation.

These articles of merger were signed by the corporation on ____November 10, 1998____.

By: _____*Raymond Rodriguez*_____

Raymond Rodriguez, President

DISSENTING SHAREHOLDERS

See the discussion of dissenters' rights in chapter 10. The merger of a corporation is one of those fundamental changes that will give rise to dissenters' rights, and it must be dealt with carefully and cautiously for the reasons discussed earlier.

EXCHANGING STOCK CERTIFICATES

Where, as in the hypothetical above, the shareholders of the merging corporation will be getting shares of the surviving corporation in connection with the merger, you will want to retrieve their old certificates and replace them with certificates for the correct number of shares of the surviving corporation. On the following page is an example of a request that the old certificates be sent in for exchange. You'll note in the plan of merger that, even if the shareholders don't cooperate, the old share certificates nevertheless represent shares of the surviving corporation once the merger is effective.

Alternate letter requesting the exchange of old certificates—

Scrupulous America, Inc.

400 West 61st Avenue, P.O. Box 19, New York, NY 10032

Henry Hardy
1440 Enterprise Blvd.
New York, NY 10033

Re: Share certificate(s) number(s): 000005

Dear Mr. Hardy:

Recently the shareholders of Home Safety Systems, Inc., voted to merge the company into Scrupulous America, Inc. Under the terms of the merger, each outstanding share of Home Safety Systems, Inc., was exchanged for one share of Scrupulous America, Inc. The merger is now complete, and your corporation would like to exchange your certificate(s) representing shares of Home Safety Systems, Inc., for new certificate(s) representing shares of Scrupulous America, Inc.

Enclosed for your convenience is an envelope addressed to the corporate secretary. Please place your certificates in the envelope and return them to the company. No postage is required. The Secretary will issue new share certificates representing the appropriate number of shares of Scrupulous America, Inc., in the same name or names as the old ones and send them to you by return mail to the address listed above. If you would like the certificates sent to a different address, please so indicate by changing the above address as appropriate and returning this letter to us along with your old shares.

Thank you for your cooperation.

Scrupulous America, Inc.

By: *Raymond Rodriguez*
Raymond Rodriguez, President

Other Methods
of Acquiring
a Business

13

Other than mergers, stock purchases and asset purchases are the usual methods of acquiring a business. In a stock purchase, the acquirer will simply purchase most or all of the outstanding shares of a corporation. In the usual form, this means that the purchaser will negotiate the transaction with each existing shareholder of the target business. It works well if there is only one or a few shareholders, but presents obvious difficulties if there are many. Most states now allow a *share exchange* procedure in which the shareholders of the target vote on whether to sell their shares as a group. The procedure is very much like that for a merger (including dissenters' rights). It can also be accomplished through a tender offer (see page 167).

In an asset purchase, the acquirer buys most or all of the things owned by the target business and uses the assets to continue the business, leaving behind a shell, more or less. The great thing about an asset purchase is that the buyer can pick and choose what it wants and leave behind the undesirable parts, including liabilities.

Stock purchases and asset purchases may sound simpler than mergers, but don't be deceived. The tax implications are at least as complex and, although you may avoid a shareholders vote in a stock or asset transaction, you may not. A share exchange will require the same sort of vote that a merger would. And if a corporation sells all or substantially all its assets except "in the ordinary course of business," that too requires shareholder approval.

STOCK TRANSACTIONS

BUYING THE
OUTSTANDING
SHARES

The usual stock transaction involves one corporation buying all the outstanding shares of another from one or several shareholders. The procedure is not different in concept from the procedure you would use to buy a house. After looking over the purchase and deciding it is what you want, you negotiate a deal.

Frequently there is a *letter of intent*, a sort of preliminary agreement, sometimes called an *agreement in principle*, laying out the basic terms of the deal which serves as a sort of verbal handshake. It may be a legally binding contract even though it is short and informal, so treat it with respect. It may have legal consequences, so don't sign it unless you mean it.

Once there is an "agreement to agree" embodied in the letter of intent, your lawyers will negotiate a more detailed "definitive agreement" which will cover the items mentioned in the letter of intent and many others besides.

The final decision to buy will have to be made by the board of directors in a resolution such as the one on the following page. Of course, management will have kept the directors fully informed of the negotiations throughout the process, and may want the directors to specifically authorize each step by appropriate resolutions.

R-63. Directors' resolution authorizing acquisition—

WHEREAS, the management of the corporation has entered into negotiations with **[name of seller]** for the sale and purchase of the outstanding shares of **[target corporation]** by this company, and after due consideration the directors have determined that such transaction under the terms and conditions expressed in the "Stock Acquisition Agreement" presented to the directors at this meeting (a copy of the Agreement referred to is located in Management Storage file No. **[file number]**) is in the best interests of the Corporation, it is therefore,

RESOLVED, that the purchase of the outstanding shares of **[target corporation]** by this company under the terms and conditions of the Stock Acquisition Agreement executed by management dated **[date of agreement]** is hereby approved, ratified and confirmed, and further

RESOLVED, that the appropriate officers of the corporation are authorized and directed to take such actions as may be necessary to give effect to the foregoing resolutions.

TENDER OFFERS

Where there are too many shareholders to negotiate a stock transaction with each of them, a tender offer may be a workable alternative. A tender offer is really a package of offers made simultaneously by a potential buyer to each individual shareholder on a take it or leave it basis, conditioned on there being enough takers to satisfy the buyer. Each shareholder decides whether or not to sell. If enough of them agree to sell, the buyer will have the number of shares it wants.

However, where there are so many shareholders that individual negotiations are impractical, the tender offer procedure may become an expensive proposition richly complicated in its own right. Tender offers are highly regulated by the Securities and Exchange Commission and by state governments.

ASSET TRANSACTIONS

BUYING THE
ASSETS OF A
CORPORATION

In an asset transaction, instead of buying a batch of identical things—shares of stock—you are buying a list of individual items—desks, computers, paper clips, trucks. It may be that some of these assets are transferable only by way of special documentation. For example, if you are buying the target's fleet of automobiles, you have to deal with the title documents peculiar to motor vehicles. If you are buying the target's real estate, deeds must be recorded, and if you are buying shares of stock that the target owns, the share certificates must be endorsed and the transfer recorded by the issuing corporation. So an asset transaction may involve a formidable stack of documents.

Nevertheless, the same basic documents involved in a typical stock transaction will be somewhere in the stack.

If the seller is a corporation disposing of all or substantially all of its assets, the transaction will have to be approved by the seller's shareholders in much the same way that they would have to approve a merger or share exchange.

R-64.   Directors' resolution authorizing acquisition—

WHEREAS, the management of the corporation has entered into negotiations with [name of seller] for the sale and purchase of substantially all of the assets of [target corporation] by this company, and after due consideration the directors have determined that such transaction under the terms and conditions expressed in the "Asset Acquisition Agreement" presented to the directors at this meeting (a copy of the Agreement referred to is located in Management Storage file No. [file number]), it is therefore,

RESOLVED, that the purchase of the assets of [target corporation] by this company under the terms and conditions of the Asset Acquisition Agreement executed by management dated [date of agreement] is hereby approved, ratified and confirmed, and further

RESOLVED, that the appropriate officers of the corporation are authorized and directed to take such actions as may be necessary to give effect to the foregoing resolutions including without limitation the recordation of deeds and other documents of title as may be necessary or desirable to effect the transfer of ownership of the assets purchased.

BULK SALES   One of the advantages of an asset transaction mentioned above is that the buyer can leave undesirable assets and liabilities of the seller behind and purchase only the assets the buyer really wants. This is in contrast to a merger or stock acquisition in which the buyer acquires the target warts and all, becoming responsible for the target's liabilities at the same time it acquires the target's assets. There is a danger then, that in an asset deal, a corporation might keep its debts while giving up all the assets it could use to pay the debts, thus cheating its creditors. The states have enacted *bulk sales* statutes as a safeguard for creditors in such situations. The statutes require that a company selling most of its assets must give fair notice to its creditors so they can take steps to protect themselves. If the requirements of the statute are not followed precisely, the buyer will find itself responsible for the seller's debts whether it wants them or not.

DISSENTING   As with mergers and share exchanges, shareholders of a corporation
SHAREHOLDERS   selling substantially all of its assets will have dissenters' rights. See chapter 10.

FINANCIAL TRANSACTIONS 14

TAX STATUS

If your corporation is currently registered as a "C" corporation, and you want to change it to an "S" corporation, the IRS Form 2553 for making this election is included in appendix B as Form 48. If you change the corporation's tax status, the directors should probably adopt a resolution for the change. Be sure to consult your tax adviser before changing the tax status.

BORROWING MONEY

Like other people, corporations sometimes need more money than they have and must borrow money from a bank or a friend. The procedure is little different from the procedure an individual follows in doing the same thing.

BORROWING FROM AN INSTITUTION — When the corporation goes to a bank for a loan, the bank will usually insist on using its own standard form documents right down to a standard form resolution for the directors to vote on authorizing the loan. The forms given below are much shorter and less formal that standard bank forms are likely to be, and are more suitable for smaller loans such as might be obtained by a small company from one of its shareholders.

POSSIBLE When a corporation borrows from a "friend," that is, a shareholder or
CONFLICTS director, some potential conflicts arise. The company and the director or shareholder must be careful to avoid potential liability (see chapter 9). With the right context, such as that provided with the purchase of property from a director (see chapter 9), the following resolution may be used in borrowing from a director, shareholder or other person.

R-65.   **Directors' resolution authorizing the borrowing of money—**

RESOLVED, that the corporation shall borrow from [name of lender] the sum of $[amount of loan] at the rate of interest and payable according to and subject to the other terms and conditions of a promissory note presented to the directors for their approval (located in Management Storage File No. [file number]), and further

RESOLVED, that the president or vice president and secretary or assistant secretary of the corporation are hereby authorized and directed to execute such note under the seal of the corporation, to receive the proceeds of such loan, and to deposit such proceeds into the depository accounts of the corporation, and to take such other actions as may be necessary or desirable to give effect to these resolutions.

LOANING MONEY

The primary lending done by small corporations is the lending of money to officers and directors. Such lending should not be undertaken lightly. Lending money to a shareholder may be considered a distribution of corporate assets and may be subject to the same limitations as dividends (see chapter 6). Moreover, it is an unequal distribution (that is, some shareholders get it and some don't) and may be subject to legal limitations for that reason. Such distributions may also have surprising and unwelcome tax effects. Lending to officers and directors may be a conflict of interest and subject the borrowers to liability for a breach of their fiduciary duty to the corporation. Therefore, it would be a good idea to consult an attorney and tax accountant before making such loans.

R-66. Directors' resolution authorizing loan to officer or director—

> RESOLVED, that the **[corporate officer other than the borrower]** is hereby authorized to issue a check to **[name of borrower]** for the sum of $**[amount]** upon receipt of a promissory note [and financing statement if collateral is to be pledged] signed by the borrower providing for the payment of interest at the rate of **[percentage rate]** per cent per annum **[or other terms as may be agreed upon]**.

BUYING AND SELLING REAL ESTATE

PREPARING FOR
THE SALE AND
PURCHASE

Unless the business of your corporation is the purchase, development and resale or leasing of real property, it is likely that the decision to buy or sell land or buildings represents a significant step. It will follow careful, and possibly quite lengthy, consideration including a period of investigation, appraisal and thought about the future of the business. The issue may be visited several times by the board of directors which may want to be involved at every step.

Eventually the final decision will be made and the authority of the board of directors to complete the transaction will be needed. On the following page is a directors' resolution authorizing the purchase of real property with the proceeds of a bank loan. It presumes that the directors have previously authorized the company's officers to negotiate the purchase and enter into contracts subject to the board's final approval. On page 174, is a resolution authorizing the sale of real property.

R-67. **Directors' resolution authorizing the purchase of real property—**

WHEREAS, management of the corporation, under authority previously given by this board of directors, have entered into negotiations for the purchase of real property located at **[address or other description of the property]** and have recommended to the directors that the corporation agree to the purchase of such property for the sum of $**[purchase price]** under the terms and conditions contained in a "Contract for the Sale and Purchase of Real Property" dated **[date of contract]** (a copy of such contract is located in management storage file no. **[file number]**), and

WHEREAS, management has recommended that the company purchase such property using the proceeds of a loan negotiated by management from **[name of lender]** under the terms and conditions of a "Loan Agreement" dated **[date of loan agreement]** (management storage file no. **[file number]**), and

WHEREAS, after due consideration, the board of directors believes such transactions to be in the best interests of the corporation, it is therefore,

RESOLVED, that the "Contract for the Sale and Purchase of Real Property" dated **[date]** between **[name of seller]** and the corporation and the "Loan Agreement" dated **[date]** between **[name of lender]** and the corporation presented to this board for its consideration are hereby approved, ratified and confirmed, and further,

RESOLVED, that the appropriate officers of the corporation are authorized and directed, with the advice of corporate legal counsel, to execute other documents, including without limitation notes, mortgages and deeds of trust, in order to complete the described borrowing of funds and purchase of real property according to the terms of such agreements, and to take such further actions as may be necessary or desirable to give effect to the foregoing resolutions.

R-68.   Directors' resolution authorizing the sale of real property—

WHEREAS, management of the corporation, under authority previously given by this board of directors, have entered into negotiations for the sale of real property belonging to the company located at **[address or other description of the property]** and have recommended to the directors that the corporation agree to the sale of such property for the amount of **[sale price]** under the terms and conditions contained in a "Contract for the Sale and Purchase of Real Property" dated **[date of contract]** (a copy of such contract is located in management storage file no. **[file number]**), and

WHEREAS, after due consideration, the board of directors believes such transaction to be in the best interests of the corporation, it is therefore,

RESOLVED, that the "Contract for the Sale and Purchase of Real Property" dated **[date]** between the corporation and **[name of buyer]** presented to this board for its consideration is hereby approved, ratified and confirmed, and further,

RESOLVED, that the appropriate officers of the corporation are authorized and directed, with the advice of corporate legal counsel, to execute other documents, including without limitation a deed for the transfer of such property, in order to complete the described sale of real property according to the terms of such agreement, and to take such further actions as may be necessary or desirable to give effect to the foregoing resolutions.

CONTRACTS,
DEEDS, AND
LAWYERS

Buying and selling real estate has been going on for thousands of years. One of the reasons we developed law in the first place was to protect the ownership of real estate without the need for armed combat. So the laws are hoary and, like the lands they deal with, are uniquely tied to and vary with the jurisdiction. A lawyer who knows the applicable state law and even the recording customs at the local court house will be indispensable even for small real estate transactions. He or she will know what to do about title searches, insurance and countless little details that will nevertheless loom large if not handled correctly. For more information, *How to Negotiate Real Estate Contracts*, by Mark Warda (also published by Sourcebooks, Inc.).

CLOSING THE
SALE

A real estate closing can be a monumental paper shuffle, especially if the property is complex commercial property. Once again the value of an attorney experienced in the procedure will be indispensable. But you have a part, too. Keep an eye on the detail. Before the closing, become as familiar as you can with the documents that will pass under your nose. You know what's important to you better than your lawyer can. There won't be much time for reading and explanations at the closing, and what there is you will likely be paying for by the hour.

LEASING REAL ESTATE

Leasing real property is a lot like buying it. In fact you are buying it for a period of time, so the process is in some ways similar. Commercial real estate leases are usually quite long and vary considerably with the nature of the property involved, so there is no use trying to include a sample in this book.

AUTHORIZATION

As with a purchase, any lease of real property is going to be an important event for the company that will require the directors' approval.

R-69.   Directors' resolution to lease real property—

WHEREAS, management of the corporation, under authority previously given by this board of directors, have entered into negotiations for the long term lease of real property located at **[address or other description of the property]** and have recommended to the directors that the corporation agree to the lease of such property under the terms and conditions contained in a "Contract for the lease of Real Property" dated **[date of contract]** (a copy of such contract is located in management storage file no. **[file number]**), and

WHEREAS, after due consideration, the board of directors believes such transaction to be in the best interests of the corporation, it is therefore,

---

> RESOLVED, that the "Contract for the Lease of Real Property"
> dated **[date]** between **[name of lessor]** and the corporation presented to
> this board for its consideration is hereby approved, ratified and
> confirmed, and further,
>
> RESOLVED, that the appropriate officers of the corporation are
> authorized and directed, to take such further actions as may be
> necessary or desirable to give effect to the foregoing resolu-
> tions.

For more information about real estate leases, see *How to Negotiate Real Estate Leases*, by Mark Warda (also published by Sourcebooks, Inc.).

SELLING AND PURCHASING EQUIPMENT

This, and the following, section is written mostly for the benefit of the business that occasionally purchases or leases equipment for its own use, and occasionally disposes of such equipment. The implications of selling and leasing equipment as a business are beyond the scope of this book.

Not every purchase or sale of equipment requires formal authorization by a company's board of directors. It depends on the size of the corporation compared to the size of the transaction being considered. It's not likely that the board of directors of a multi-million dollar corporation would concern itself with the purchase of one copy machine. It depends on the customary relationship between the board and management. What does the board expect? Would it be surprised to hear that management had made the proposed purchase without consulting the board? It may also depend simply on whether or not the other party to the contract wants assurance of the board's approval.

Below is a resolution granting the board's approval. Remember that directors can approve of management's actions after the fact. If it's only after a transaction takes place that management gets around to asking permission, and if the board is of a mind to give belated permission, the same form works. In addition to *approving* the board also *ratifies*.

There is really no conceptual difference between the board's approval of equipment sales and purchases and approval of sales and purchases of real estate. The following resolution is shorter than the ones above dealing with real estate, only for the reason that equipment transactions are ordinarily smaller than real estate transactions. But if a particular equipment deal is as important to the company as buying and selling real estate would ordinarily be, then you may want to use the more elaborate forms as a guide.

R-70.   Directors' resolution to purchase (sell) equipment—

WHEREAS, management of the corporation have recommended to the directors that the corporation agree to the **[purchase/sale]** of **[description of equipment]** for the sum of $**[purchase price]** under the terms and conditions contained in a Contract dated **[date of contract]** (a copy of such contract is located in management storage file no. **[file number]**), and

WHEREAS, after due consideration, the board of directors believes such transaction to be in the best interests of the corporation, it is therefore,

RESOLVED, that the Contract dated **[date]** between **[name of seller]** and the corporation presented to this board for its consideration are hereby approved, ratified and confirmed, and further,

RESOLVED, that the appropriate officers of the corporation are hereby authorized and directed to take such further actions as may be necessary or desirable to give effect to the foregoing resolutions.

LEASING EQUIPMENT

Sometimes equipment leasing arrangements are really an alternative method of financing the purchase of equipment. The lessee "leases" the equipment but expects that, at the end of the lease term, ownership of the property will transfer to the lessee. The tax treatment of such arrangements is a complicated subject that can't be dealt with here. The transactions discussed here are relatively short term rental arrangements of needed equipment which the renter will, after the rental term, return to its owner.

The decision about whether or not director approval of a rental agreement is needed is based on the same considerations discussed above in connection with the sale and purchase of equipment.

R-71.   Directors' resolution to rent equipment—

WHEREAS, management of the corporation have recommended to the directors that the corporation agree to the rental of **[description of equipment]** under the terms and conditions contained in a Rental Agreement dated **[date of agreement]** (a copy of such contract is located in management storage file no. **[file number]**), and

WHEREAS, after due consideration, the board of directors believes such transaction to be in the best interests of the corporation, it is therefore,

RESOLVED, that the Rental Agreement dated **[date]** between **[name of lessor]** and the corporation presented to this board for its consideration are hereby approved, ratified and confirmed, and further,

RESOLVED, that the appropriate officers of the corporation are hereby authorized and directed to take such further actions as may be necessary or desirable to give effect to the foregoing resolutions.

ASSIGNMENT OF ASSETS FROM SHAREHOLDER

Sometimes a shareholder will contribute assets, instead of cash, to the corporation. Form 50 is an Assignment of Assets form to accomplish such a transfer. Of course, if the property being transferred is of a certain nature, you may also need to take whatever steps are necessary to legally transfer title. Also, before engaging in any such transfer, you may want to obtain the advice of your tax adviser.

APPENDIX A
DIRECTORY OF STATE
CORPORATE STATUTES

The following information gives the citation to the corporation statutes or code of each state. The names of the statutes or code are those which appear on the books. In some states the name of the publisher is included in the title (such as *West's* Colorado Revised Statutes Annotated or *Vernon's* Annotated Missouri Statutes). For those states that have volume numbers printed on the spine of the books, the volume number is also given below to help you locate the law (however, these are the volume numbers as of the date of publication, and they may change from year to year). If you have any difficulty finding the corporation law for your state, ask a librarian to help you locate it.

Alabama:
Code of Alabama, Title 10-2A

Alaska:
Alaska Statutes, Title 10 (volume 2)

Arizona:
Arizona Revised Statutes Annotated, Title 10 (1994 supplement to volume 3)

Arkansas:
Arkansas Code of 1987 Annotated, Title 4, Chapter 27 (volume 2A)

California:
West's Annotated California Code (look for volume titled "Corporations")

Colorado:
West's Colorado Revised Statutes Annotated, Title 7

Connecticut:
Connecticut General Statutes Annotated, Title 33

Delaware:
Delaware Code Annotated, Title 8

District of Columbia:
District of Columbia Code, Title 29

Florida:
Florida Statutes, Chapter 607 (volume 4)

Georgia:
Official Code of Georgia Annotated, Title 14 (volume 12) [Note: This is not the "Georgia Code," which is a separate, outdated set of books with a different numbering system.]

Hawaii:
Hawaii Revised Statutes Annotated, Title 23, Chapter 415 (volume 8)

Idaho:
Idaho Code, Title 30 (volume 5B)

Illinois:
West's Smith Hurd Illinois Compiled Statutes Annotated, Chapter 805 (1994 supplement)

Indiana:
West's Indiana Statutes Annotated, Title 23, Article 1

Iowa:
Iowa Code Annotated, Chapter 490 (volume 26)

Kansas:
Kansas Statutes Annotated-Official, Chapter 17 (volume 2); OR
Vernon's Kansas Statutes Annotated, Section 17-6001 et seq. (volume 5 titled "General Corporation Code")

Kentucky:
Kentucky Revised Statutes, Chapter 271B (volume 10A)

Louisiana:
West's LSA Revised Statutes, Section 12-174 et seq. (volume 5)

Maine:
Maine Revised Statutes Annotated, Title 13-A (volume 6A)

Maryland:
Annotated Code of Maryland (volume titled
"Corporations and Associations")

Massachusetts:
Annotated Laws of Massachusetts, Chapter 156

Michigan:
Michigan Statutes Annotated, Section 21.1 et seq.; OR
Michigan Compiled Laws Annotated, Section 450.1 et seq.

Minnesota:
Minnesota Statutes Annotated, Chapter 302A (volume 20)

Mississippi:
Mississippi Code 1972 Annotated, Title 79

Missouri:
Vernon's Annotated Missouri Statutes, Section 351 (volume 17A)

Montana:
Montana Code Annotated, Title 35 (volume 7)

Nebraska:
Revised Statutes of Nebraska, Chapter 21 (volume 1A)

Nevada:
Nevada Revised Statutes Annotated, Chapter 78 (volume 2A)

New Hampshire:
New Hampshire Revised Statutes
    Annotated, Chapter 293-A (ignore
    "Title" numbers)

New Jersey:
NJSA (for "New Jersey Statutes
    Annotated"), Title 14A (volume 14A
    titled "Corporations, General")

New Mexico:
New Mexico Statutes 1978 Annotated,
    Chapter 53 (volume 9)

New York:
McKinney's Consolidated Laws of New
    York
Annotated (volume 6 titled "Business
    Corporation")

North Carolina:
North Carolina General Statutes, Chapter
    55 (volume 9) [Note: The actual title
    on the cover of the set of books is
    "The General Statutes of North
    Carolina"]

North Dakota:
North Dakota Century Code Annotated,
    Title 10 (volume 2A)

Ohio:
Page's Ohio Revised Code Annotated,
    Title 17

Oklahoma:
Oklahoma Statutes Annotated, Title 18

Oregon:
Oregon Revised Statutes Annotated,
    Chapter 60 (volume 4)

Pennsylvania:
Purdon's Pennsylvania Statutes Annotated,
    Title 15

Puerto Rico:
Puerto Rico Laws Annotated, Title 14

Rhode Island:
General Laws of Rhode Island,
    Section 7-1.1 (volume 2B)

South Carolina:
Code of Laws of South Carolina, Title 33
    (volume 10A)

South Dakota:
South Dakota Codified Laws, Title 47
    (volume 14)

Tennessee:
Tennessee Code Annotated, Title 48
    (volume 8B)

Texas:
Vernon's Texas Civil Statutes, Business
    Corporation Act (volume 3A)

Utah:
Utah Code Annotated, Title 16
    (volume 2B)

Vermont:
Vermont Statutes Annotated, Title 11A

Virginia:
Code of Virginia 1950, Title 13 (volume 3)

Washington:
West's Revised Code of Washington
    Annotated, Title 23B

West Virginia:
West Virginia Code, Chapter 13
    (volume 5)

Wisconsin:
West's Wisconsin Statutes Annotated,
    Section 180

Wyoming:
Wyoming Statutes Annotated, Title 17
    (volume 5)

APPENDIX B
FORMS

This appendix contains the blank forms to use for your corporation. Below is a list of the forms found in this appendix, with the form number (found in the upper, outside corner of the form), the name of the form, and the page on which it can be found. For some of the forms (especially minutes and resolutions) you will need to insert various provisions from the main part of the book. To help you locate these provisions, see the table on page 9.

Forms Directory

Minutes of Regular Meeting of
the Board of Directors of

_____

      A meeting of the Board of Directors of the Corporation was held on the date and at the time and place set forth in the written notice of meeting, or waiver of notice signed by directors, and attached to the minutes of this meeting.

      The following directors were present: _____

_____.

      The meeting was called to order and it was moved, seconded and carried that _____ act as Chairman and that _____ act as Secretary.

      Minutes of the preceding meeting of the Board, held on _____, were read and approved.

      Upon motion duly made, seconded and carried, the following resolution(s) was/were adopted:

❑ See attached resolutions.

      There being no further business, the meeting adjourned.

_____
Secretary

Approved:

_____

Minutes of Special Meeting of
the Board of Directors of

_____

A special meeting of the Board of Directors of the Corporation was held on the date and at the time and place set forth in the written notice of meeting, or waiver of notice signed by directors, and attached to the minutes of this meeting.

The following directors were present: _____

_____.

The meeting was called to order and it was moved, seconded and carried that _____ act as Chairman and that _____ act as Secretary.

Minutes of the preceding meeting of the Board, held on _____, were read and approved.

Upon motion duly made, seconded and carried, the following resolution(s) was/were adopted:

❏ See attached resolutions.

There being no further business, the meeting adjourned.

_____
Secretary

Approved:

_____

Directors Meeting Minutes Continuation Sheet

Type & Date of Meeting:_____

Page_____ of _____ pages.

Consent to Action Without Formal Meeting of Directors of

_____

The undersigned, being all of the Directors of the Corporation, hereby adopt the following resolutions:

❏ See attached resolutions.

RESOLVED, that these resolutions shall be effective at _____ ____.m.,
on_____, _____.

_____
Director

_____
Director

_____
Director

_____
Director

_____
Director

_____
Director

Minutes of the Annual Meeting of
the Shareholders of

_____

The annual meeting of the Shareholders of the Corporation was held on the date and at the time and place set forth in the written notice of meeting, or waiver of notice signed by shareholders, and attached to the minutes of this meeting.

The following shareholders were present:

Shareholder   No. of Shares

_____   _____

_____   _____

_____   _____

_____   _____

_____   _____

_____   _____

The meeting was called to order and it was moved, seconded and carried that _____ _____ act as Chairman and that _____ act as Secretary.

A roll call was taken and the Chairman noted that all of the outstanding shares of the Corporation were represented in person or by proxy. Any proxies are attached to these minutes.

Minutes of the preceding meeting of the Shareholders, held on _____, were read and approved.

Upon motion duly made, seconded and carried, the following were elected directors for the following year:

_____   _____

_____   _____

❏ See attached resolutions.

There being no further business, the meeting adjourned.

_____
Secretary

Approved:

_____

Minutes of Special Meeting of
the Shareholders of

_____

A special meeting of the Shareholders of the Corporation was held on the date and at the time and place set forth in the written notice of meeting, or waiver of notice signed by shareholders, and attached to the minutes of this meeting.

The following shareholders were present:

Shareholder	No. of Shares
_____	_____
_____	_____
_____	_____
_____	_____
_____	_____
_____	_____

The meeting was called to order and it was moved, seconded and carried that _____ _____ act as Chairman and that _____ act as Secretary.

A roll call was taken and the Chairman noted that all of the outstanding shares of the Corporation were represented in person or by proxy. Any proxies are attached to these minutes.

Minutes of the preceding meeting of the Shareholders, held on _____, were read and approved.

Upon motion duly made, seconded and carried, the following resolution(s) was/were adopted:

❑ See attached resolutions.

There being no further business, the meeting adjourned.

_____
Secretary

Shareholders:

_____

Shareholders Meeting Minutes Continuation Sheet

Type & Date of Meeting:_____

Page_____ of _____ pages.

Consent to Action Without Formal Meeting of Shareholders of

_____

The undersigned, being all of the shareholders of the Corporation, hereby adopt the following resolutions:

❏ See attached resolutions.

RESOLVED, that these resolutions shall be effective at _____ ____.m., on_____, _____.

_____
Shareholder

_____
Shareholder

_____
Shareholder

_____
Shareholder

_____
Shareholder

_____
Shareholder

_____
Shareholder

_____
Shareholder

Resolution of the Board of Directors of

_____

Date:_____

At the meeting referenced above, the Board of Directors hereby adopts the following resolution (which shall be attached to and incorporated by reference in the minutes of said meeting):

Resolution of the Shareholders of

_____

Date:_____

At the meeting referenced above, the Shareholders hereby adopt the following resolution (which shall be attached to and incorporated by reference in the minutes of said meeting):

Certified Copy of Minutes of Meeting
of the Board of Directors of

_____

    I HEREBY CERTIFY that I am the Corporate Secretary of _____

_____, that the following is an accurate copy of minutes of a

meeting of the Board of Directors of _____,

held on _____, _____:

    ❏ See attached minutes and/or resolutions.

Signed and the seal of the Corporation affixed, _____, _____.

_____

Secretary

Certified Copy of Minutes of Meeting
of the Shareholders of

_____

    I HEREBY CERTIFY that I am the Corporate Secretary of _____

_____, that the following is an accurate copy of minutes of a

meeting of the Shareholders of _____,

held on _____, _____:

    ❏ See attached minutes and/or resolutions.

Signed and the seal of the Corporation affixed, _____, _____.

_____

Secretary

Certified Copy of Resolutions Adopted by
the Board of Directors of

_____

      I HEREBY CERTIFY that I am the Corporate Secretary of _____

_____, that the following is an accurate copy of resolution(s) adopted by the Board of Directors of _____, effective _____, _____, and that such resolutions continue in effect as of the date of this certification:

    ❑ See attached resolutions.

Signed and the seal of the Corporation affixed, _____, _____.

_____

                      Secretary

Certified Copy of Resolutions Adopted by
the Shareholders of

_____

    I HEREBY CERTIFY that I am the Corporate Secretary of _____

_____, that the following is an accurate copy of resolution(s)

adopted by the Shareholders of _____, effec-

tive _____, _____, and that such resolutions continue in effect as of the

date of this certification:

    ❏ See attached resolutions.

Signed and the seal of the Corporation affixed, _____, _____.

_____

               Secretary

Director's Consent to Serve

Date:

TO: The Board of Directors

_____

[name of corporation]

I hereby consent to serve as a director of the Corporation, if elected.

_____

Certification of Secretary of

_____

I HEREBY CERTIFY that I am the Corporate Secretary of _____

_____, that the individuals listed below are the duly elected

directors of the Corporation, and that they continue to hold the office of director on the date of

this certification:

Signed and the seal of the Corporation affixed, _____, _____.

_____

Secretary

Notice of Regular Meeting of the Board of Directors of

_____

Date:

TO: All Directors

The regular meeting of the board of directors will be held on _____,
_____, at _____ ___.m., at _____
_____.

_____

Corporate Secretary

Notice of Special Meeting of the Board of Directors of

_____

Date:

TO: All Directors

There will be a special meeting of the board of directors on _____,

_____, at _____ ___.m., at _____

_____.

The purpose(s) of this meeting is/are:

_____

Corporate Secretary

Waiver of Notice of Meeting of Board of Directors of

_____

The undersigned director(s) of the Corporation hereby waive any and all notice required by law or by the articles of incorporation or bylaws of the Corporation, and consent to the holding of a ❑ Regular ❑ Special   meeting of the Board of Directors of the Corporation on _____, at _____ ____.m., at _____.

Name:_____   Date:_____

Name:_____   Date:_____

Name:_____   Date:_____

Name:_____   Date:_____

Name:_____   Date:_____

Name:_____   Date:_____

Agenda of Meeting of the Board of Directors of

Date of Meeting:_____

Certificate No.:_____

No. of Shares:_____

_____

Incorporated under the laws of the State of _____

Authorized Capital Stock:_____ shares.

Par Value: ❑ $_____ per Share   ❑ No Par Value

     THIS CERTIFIES THAT _____ is
the owner of _____ fully paid and nonassessable shares of the capital
stock of _____transferable
only on the books of the corporation by the holder of this certificate in person or by the holder's
duly authorized attorney upon surrender of this certificate properly endorsed.

     Upon request, and without charge, the corporation will provide written information as to
the designations, preferences, limitations, and relative rights of all classes and series of shares and
the authority of the board of directors to determine the same for future classes and series.

     IN WITNESS WHEREOF, _____has
caused this certificate to be signed by its duly authorized officers and its corporate seal to be
affixed on _____.

                               _____ , President

_____, Secretary

FOR VALUE RECEIVED, the undersigned hereby sells, assigns and transfers to

_____,

_____ of the shares represented by the certificate on the reverse side, and irrevocably

appoints _____ attorney, with full power of

substitution, to transfer such shares on the books of the Corporation.

_____

Witness:

_____

Social Security Account Number or other Taxpayer Identification Number of the

assignee:_____

Stock Subscription Agreement

_____

In consideration of the mutual promises contained in this agreement and other lawful and sufficient consideration, the receipt of which is hereby acknowledged, _____ _____ (the "Corporation"), a _____corporation, agrees to issue, and the undersigned purchaser agrees to subscribe to and purchase _____ shares of the _____ of the Corporation for cash at the price of \$_____. The purchase price for the shares shall be payable in full upon issuance of the shares by the Corporation.

Purchaser:_____

_____

(Name, address, and social security number of taxpayer identification number of purchaser)

_____

(Signature of Purchaser)

Corporation:

By:_____

Stock Option Agreement

_____

In consideration of the mutual promises contained in this agreement and other lawful consideration, the receipt and sufficiency of which is hereby acknowledged, _____(the "Corporation), a _____ corporation, hereby grants to _____ (the "Grantee") an option to purchase shares of the Corporation upon the following terms and conditions:

1. **Consideration of the Grantee.** The grant of an option in this agreement is made in consideration of _____

_____.

2. **Number of shares and price.** The option granted in this agreement (the "Option") is an option of the Grantee to purchase _____ shares of the _____ _____ shares of the Corporation. The purchase price of the shares will be $_____ per share, payable in cash upon the exercise of the option.

3. **Time and method of exercise.** The Option may be exercised in whole or in part by the Grantee at any time and from time to time before _____ by delivery to the Corporation at its principal office written notice of the Grantee's intent to exercise the option stating the number of shares being purchased and accompanied by the purchase price of the shares being purchased. The option may be exercised as to whole numbers of shares only.

4. **Adjustments of the number of shares subject to the Option.** In the event of any share dividend, share split or other recapitalization affecting the shares of the Company, or a merger of the Corporation in which it is the surviving corporation, the number of shares subject to the Option will be automatically adjusted to equitably reflect such change or merger. In the event of the dissolution of the Corporation, or a merger or other fundamental change following which no shares of the corporation may be issued, the Option will terminate, but the Grantee will have a reasonable opportunity to exercise the Option immediately before such event. Except as provided in this paragraph, the Grantee shall have no rights as a shareholder of the Corporation with respect to the shares subject to the Option until such shares are issued upon exercise of the Option.

5. **No transfer.** The Option may not be transferred by the Grantee other than by will or the laws of inheritance.

The Corporation and the Grantee have executed this Stock Option Agreement under seal on _____, _____.

Grantee: Corporation:

_____   By: _____ _____
                                                                                    President

                                                         Attest:

                                                         _____
                                                                            Secretary

Stock Powers Separate From Certificate

In exchange for valuable consideration, the receipt and sufficiency of which is hereby acknowledged, the undersigned hereby sells, assigns and transfers to _____ _____, _____ shares of the stock of _____ registered on the books of the Corporation in the name of the undersigned and represented by Certificate(s) number_____.

The undersigned hereby irrevocably appoints _____, _____, attorney, with full power of substitution, to transfer such shares on the books of the Corporation.

Executed on _____.

_____

(Name of person transferring stock)

Witness:

_____

Social Security Account Number of other Taxpayer Identification Number of the assignee:_____

Certificate No.:_____

No. of Preferred Shares, Series_____: _____

_____

PREFERRED STOCK, SERIES _____

Incorporated under the laws of the State of _____

Authorized Preferred Stock, Series _____: _____ shares, No Par Value.

    THIS CERTIFIES THAT _____ is the owner of _____ fully paid and nonassessable shares of the capital stock of _____ _____transferable only on the books of the corporation by the holder of this certificate in person or by the holder's duly authorized attorney upon surrender of this certificate properly endorsed.

    Upon request, and without charge, the corporation will provide written information as to the designations, preferences, limitations, and relative rights of all classes and series of shares and the authority of the board of directors to determine the same for future classes and series.

    IN WITNESS WHEREOF, _____has caused this certificate to be signed by its duly authorized officers and its corporate seal to be affixed on _____.

_____, President

_____, Secretary

FOR VALUE RECEIVED, the undersigned hereby sells, assigns and transfers to
_____,
_____ of the shares represented by the certificate on the reverse side, and irrevocably appoints _____ attorney, with full power of substitution, to transfer such shares on the books of the Corporation.

_____

Witness:

_____

Social Security Account Number or other Taxpayer Identification Number of the assignee:_____

Shareholders' Agreement

This agreement is made by and among _____
_____ (the "Corporation") and the undersigned
shareholders of the corporation (the "Shareholders" collectively, or "Shareholder" individually) on
_____.

In consideration of the premises and of the mutual promises and conditions contained in this agreement, the Corporation and the Shareholders agree for themselves, their successors and assigns, as follows:

1.   The number of directors of the corporation shall be _____. So long as he or she shall own shares in the Corporation, each Shareholder shall have the right to serve as a director of the Corporation or to designate a person to serve as director. Any such person named must be reasonably capable of performing the duties of a director.

2.   So long as he or she shall own shares in the Corporation, each shareholder shall have the right, but shall not be required, to serve as an officer of the Corporation. The compensation paid to each Shareholder during each calendar year for his or her services as an officer of the Corporation shall be equal to the compensation paid to each other Shareholder of the corporation for services as an officer. The titles and duties of each Shareholder so employed by the Corporation shall be as determined by the Board of Directors from time to time.

3.   The Shareholders shall vote their shares in such a way as to give effect to the provisions of this agreement.

4.   Every certificate representing shares owned by the parties to this agreement shall prominently bear the following legend: "The shares represented by this certificate are subject to the provisions of a Shareholders' Agreement dated _____, a copy of which is on file in, and may be examined at, the principal office of the Corporation."

IN WITNESS WHEREOF, the parties have executed this Agreement under seal on the date indicated above.

By:_____

Attest:_____

_____   _____
Shareholder   Shareholder

_____   _____
Shareholder   Shareholder

_____   _____
Shareholder   Shareholder

Lost or Destroyed Stock Certificate Indemnity Agreement and Affidavit

The undersigned, being duly sworn, hereby affirms the following:

1. The undersigned is record holder of _____ shares (the "Shares") of the stock of _____

(the "Corporation"). The Shares were represented by stock certificate number _____ issued on _____ (the "Certificate").

2. The undersigned is the sole owner of the Shares, having never endorsed, delivered, transferred, assigned, or otherwise disposed of them or the Certificate in such a way as to give any other person any interest in the Shares.

3. The undersigned has duly searched for the Certificate, has been unable to find it, and believes the Certificate to be lost, destroyed, or stolen.

4. In order to induce the Corporation to issue a new stock certificate to replace the Certificate, the undersigned agrees to indemnify, defend, and hold harmless the Corporation, its shareholders, directors, and officers from any and all claims, loss, or damage whatsoever arising out of or related in any manner to the Certificate or arising out of the issuance of a replacement certificate.

Dated: _____

_____

STATE OF
COUNTY OF

On _____, _____, there personally appeared before me,
_____, who ❑ is personally known to
me ❑ produced _____ as identification, and being duly
sworn on oath stated that the facts stated in the above Affidavit are true.

_____
Notary Public
My Commission Expires:

President's Call for Special Meeting of the Shareholders

To the Secretary of _____

     Pursuant to Article _____, Section _____ of the bylaws of the Corporation, there is hereby called a special meeting of the shareholders of the Corporation to be held on _____, at _____ ____.m., at _____ _____, for the following purpose(s):

     You are hereby authorized and directed to give such notice of the meeting to shareholders of record on _____ as may be required by law and the bylaws of the Corporation.

Dated:_____

                                   _____

                                   President

Shareholder's Call for Special Meeting of the Shareholders

To the Secretary of _____

     Pursuant to Article _____, Section _____ of the bylaws of the Corporation, the under-signed shareholders of _____, representing not less than one-tenth of the shares entitled to vote on the issues described below, hereby call a special meeting of the shareholders of the Corporation to be held on_____ , at _____ ____.m., at _____

_____, for the following purpose(s):

     You are hereby authorized and directed to give such notice of the meeting to shareholders of record on _____ as may be required by law and the bylaws of the Corporation.

Dated:_____

                               _____
                               [Name of shareholder and no. of shares owned]

                               _____
                               [Name of shareholder and no. of shares owned]

                               _____
                               [Name of shareholder and no. of shares owned]

                               _____
                               [Name of shareholder and no. of shares owned]

Notice of Annual Meeting of the Shareholders of

_____

Date:

TO: All Shareholders

The annual meeting of the shareholders of the Corporation will be held on
_____, _____, at _____ ____.m., at _____
_____.

The purposes of the meeting are:

1.   To elect directors.

2.   To transact such business as may properly come before the meeting and any adjournment or adjournments thereof.

By order of the board of directors:

_____

Corporate Secretary

Notice of Special Meeting of the Shareholders of

_____

Date:

TO: All Shareholders

A special meeting of the shareholders of the Corporation will be held on
_____, _____, at _____ ____.m., at _____
_____.

The purposes of the meeting are:

By order of the board of directors:

_____

Corporate Secretary

Affidavit of Mailing

The undersigned, being duly sworn, hereby affirms the following:

1.   I am the Corporate Secretary of _____ _____(the "Corporation").

2.   On _____ I caused notice of the _____ meeting of the shareholders of the Corporation to be deposited in the United States Post Office at _____, in sealed envelopes, postage prepaid, addressed to each shareholder of the Corporation of record on _____ at his or her last known address as it appeared on the books of the Corporation.

3.   A copy of such notice is attached to and incorporated by reference into this affidavit.

Date:_____

_____
Secretary

STATE OF

COUNTY OF

    On _____, _____, there personally appeared before me, _____, who, being duly sworn, deposed and said that he/she is the Secretary of _____, and that the facts stated in the above Affidavit are true.

_____
Notary Public
My Commission Expires:

Shareholder's Waiver of Notice

The undersigned Shareholder(s) of _____
_____ hereby waive any and all notice required by law or
by the articles of incorporation or bylaws of the Corporation and consent to the holding of
☐ the annual   ☐ a special   meeting of the shareholders of the corporation on
_____ at _____ _____.m., at _____
_____ for the following purposes:

\
\
\
\
\
\
\
\
\
\
\
\

_____   Date:_____
Shareholder

_____   Date:_____
Shareholder

_____   Date:_____
Shareholder

_____   Date:_____
Shareholder

_____   Date:_____
Shareholder

_____   Date:_____
Shareholder

Agenda of Meeting of the Shareholders of

_____

Date of Meeting:_____

Appointment of Proxy

The undersigned Shareholder (the "Shareholder") of _____
_____ (the "Corporation") hereby appoints
_____ as proxy, with full power of substitution, for and in the name of the Shareholder to attend all shareholders meetings of the Corporation and to act, vote, and execute consents with respect to any or all shares of the Corporation belonging to the Shareholder as fully and to the same extent and effect as the Shareholder. This appointment may be revoked by the Shareholder at any time; but, if not revoked, shall continue in effect until _____.

The date of this proxy is _____.

_____
Shareholder

Appointment of Proxy

The undersigned Shareholder (the "Shareholder") of _____

_____ (the "Corporation") hereby appoints

_____ as proxy, with full power of substitu-

tion, for and in the name of the Shareholder to attend the ❑ annual ❑ special shareholders'

meeting of the Corporation to be held on _____, at

_____ ___.m., at _____,

and to act and vote at such meeting and any adjournment thereof with respect to any or all shares

of the Corporation belonging to the Shareholder as fully and to the same extent and effect as the

Shareholder. Any appointment of proxy previously made by the Shareholder for such meeting is

hereby revoked.

The date of this proxy is _____.

_____

Appointment of Proxy

The undersigned Shareholder (the "Shareholder") of _____ _____(the "Corporation") hereby appoints _____ as proxy, with full power of substitution, for and in the name of the Shareholder to attend the ❑ annual ❑ special shareholders' meeting of the Corporation to be held on _____, at _____ ____.m., at _____, and to act and vote at such meeting and any adjournment thereof with respect to any or all shares of the Corporation belonging to the Shareholder as directed below and in his or her discretion as to any other business that may properly come before the meeting or any adjournment:

Any appointment of proxy previously made by the Shareholder for such meeting is hereby revoked.

The date of this proxy is _____.

_____

Shareholder Ballot

Annual Shareholders' Meeting of

_____

Held on:_____

The undersigned shareholder and/or proxy holder votes the shares described below as follows:

FOR ELECTION OF DIRECTORS:

Name of director	Shares voted for	Shares voted against
1. _____	_____	_____
2. _____	_____	_____
3. _____	_____	_____
4. _____	_____	_____
5. _____	_____	_____
6. _____	_____	_____

Number of shares voted by the undersigned in person: _____

Number of shares voted by the undersigned as proxy: _____

Total shares voted by this ballot: _____

A copy of the proxy form(s) authorizing the undersigned to vote by proxy as above is attached to this ballot.

_____
(signature)

_____
(name printed)

Employment Agreement

This employment agreement is made by between _____

_____ (the "Employee") and

_____

(the "Corporation"). It is agreed by the Employee and the Corporation as follows:

1. The Board of Directors of the corporation has duly appointed the Employee to the office of _____ subject to the terms and conditions of this agreement.

2. Such appointment shall be effective on _____ at which time the Employee shall begin employment and assume the duties and authorities of _____.

3. The duties of the _____ shall be as follows:

4. The Employee's salary and benefits during the term of this agreement shall be as stated in this paragraph, and may be adjusted from time to time by action of the Board of Directors of the Corporation.

5. Employment pursuant to this agreement shall be:

❑　　　for a period of _____ years beginning on the effective date stated above.

❑　　　at will and may be ended by the Employee or by action of the Board of Directors of the corporation at any time and for any reason.

This agreement was executed by the Employee and by the Corporation by authority of its Board of Directors on _____.

Corporation:　　　　　　　　　　　　　　Employee:

By: _____　　　　_____

Certification of Officers by the Secretary of

_____

I hereby certify that I am the Corporate Secretary of the Corporation, that the individuals listed below have been duly elected to the offices of the Corporation appearing opposite their names, and that they continue to hold such offices on the date of this certification:

President:_____   Vice President:_____

Secretary:_____   Treasurer:_____

Other:_____   Other:_____

Signed and the seal of the corporation affixed on _____.

_____

Corporate Secretary

Limited Power of Attorney

_____ (the "Corporation")
hereby grants to _____ (the "Agent") a
limited power of attorney. As the Corporation's attorney in fact, the Agent shall have full power
and authority to undertake and perform the following on behalf of the Corporation:

By accepting this grant, the Agent agrees to act in a fiduciary capacity consistent with the
reasonable best interests of the corporation. This power of attorney may be revoked by the
Corporation at any time; however, any person dealing with the Agent as attorney in fact may rely
on this appointment until receipt of actual notice of termination.

IN WITNESS WHEREOF, the undersigned corporation has executed this power of attorney under seal and by authority of its board of directors as of the date stated above.

By: _____
President

Attest:

_____
Secretary

STATE OF
COUNTY OF

I certify that _____ personally appeared
before me on _____ and acknowledged that (s)he is Secretary of
_____ and that by authority duly
given and as the act of the corporation, the foregoing instrument was signed in its name by its
President, sealed with its corporate seal and attested by him/her as its Secretary.

_____

Notary Public
My Commission Expires:

I hereby accept the foregoing appointment as attorney in fact on _____.

_____
Attorney in Fact

General Power of Attorney

_____ (the "Corporation")
hereby grants to _____ (the "Agent") a
general power of attorney. As the Corporation's attorney in fact, the Agent shall have full power
and authority to undertake any and all acts which may be lawfully undertaken on behalf of the
corporation including but not limited to the right to buy, sell, lease, mortgage, assign, rent or otherwise dispose of any real or personal property belonging to the Corporation; to execute, accept,
undertake and perform contracts in the name of the Corporation; to deposit, endorse, or withdraw funds to or from any bank depository of the Corporation; to initiate, defend or settle legal
actions on behalf of the Corporation; and to retain any accountant, attorney or other advisor
deemed by the Agent to be necessary to protect the interests of the Corporation in relation to
such powers.

By accepting this grant, the Agent agrees to act in a fiduciary capacity consistent with the
reasonable best interests of the Corporation. This power of attorney may be revoked by the
Corporation at any time; however, any person dealing with the Agent as attorney in fact may rely
on this appointment until receipt of actual notice of termination.

IN WITNESS WHEREOF, the undersigned corporation has executed this power of attorney under seal and by authority of its board of directors as of the date stated above.

By: _____
President

Attest:

_____
Secretary

STATE OF
COUNTY OF

I certify that _____ personally
appeared before me on _____ and acknowledged that (s)he is Secretary of
_____ and that by
authority duly given and as the act of the corporation, the foregoing instrument was signed in its
name by its President, sealed with its corporate seal and attested by him/her as its Secretary.

_____
Notary Public
My Commission Expires:

I hereby accept the foregoing appointment as attorney in fact on _____.

_____
Attorney in Fact

Revocation of Power of Attorney

The appointment of _____ as the attorney in fact of the undersigned Corporation (the "Corporation") made on _____ is hereby revoked and terminated by the Corporation effective on this date.

Signed and the corporate seal affixed on _____.

By: _____

President

Attest:

_____

Secretary

Indemnification Agreement

This indemnification agreement is entered into by and between _____, (the "Corporation") and _____, (the "Director").

In consideration of the Director's consent to serve or to continue serving as a director of the Corporation and other valuable consideration, the parties agree for themselves, their successors and assigns, as follows.

1.   Subject to the terms and limitations provided in this agreement, the Corporation hereby agrees to indemnify and hold the Director harmless to the fullest extent permitted by law against the expenses, payments and liabilities described in this agreement and incurred by the Director by reason of the fact that the Director is or was a director, officer, employee or agent of the Corporation or serves or served, at the request of the Corporation, as a director, officer, partner, trustee, employee, or agent of any other enterprise or as a trustee or administrator under an employee benefit plan.

1.1. The expenses, payments and liabilities referred to above are:

1.1.1.   Reasonable expenses, including attorneys' fees, incurred by the Director in connection with any threatened, pending, or completed inquiry, proceeding, action, suit, investigation or arbitration, whether civil, criminal, or administrative, and any appeal therefrom, whether or not brought by or on behalf of the Corporation.

1.1.2.   Any payment made by the Director in satisfaction of any judgment, money decree, fine, excise tax, penalty, or reasonable settlement for which the Director became liable in any matter described in subparagraph 1.1.1 above.

1.1.3.   Reasonable expenses, including legal fees, incurred by the Director in enforcing his or her rights under this paragraph.

1.2. To the fullest extent allowed by law, the Corporation shall pay the expenses and payments described in paragraph 1.1 above in advance of the final disposition of any matter.

2. The rights of the Director hereunder shall inure to the benefit of the Director and his or her heirs, legal representative and assigns.

3.   The Director shall have the rights provided for in this agreement whether or not he or she is an officer, director, employee, or agent at the time such liabilities or expenses are imposed or incurred, and whether or not the claim asserted against the Director is based on matters that predate the execution of this agreement.

4.   The rights of the Director under this agreement are in addition to and not exclusive of any other rights to which he or she may be entitled under any statute, agreement, insurance policy, or otherwise.

5.   The Corporation agrees to use its best reasonable efforts to obtain and pay for a policy of insurance to protect and insure the Director's rights under this agreement.

IN WITNESS WHEREOF, the parties have executed this agreement under seal and by authority of its board of directors on _____, _____.

Corporation: Director:

By: _____   _____
                       President

Attest:_____, Secretary

Articles of Merger of

_____

into

_____

These Articles of Merger are submitted by _____
_____, organized under the laws of _____
(the "Surviving Corporation") for the purpose of merging its subsidiary corporation
_____, organized under the laws of
_____ (the "Merging Corporation") into the Surviving Corporation.

1. The following Plan of Merger has been duly approved by the board of directors of the surviving corporation:

Plan of Merger

A. The name of the parent corporation into which the subsidiary shall merge is _____, which shall be the Surviving Corporation, and the name of the subsidiary corporation which shall merge into the parent is _____, which shall be the Merging Corporation.

B. On the effective date of the merger, the Merging Corporation shall merge into the Surviving Corporation and the corporate existence of the Merging Corporation shall cease. The shares of the Merging Corporation shall not be converted into shares, obligations or other securities of the Surviving Corporation or any other corporation or into cash or other property in whole or in part. The outstanding shares of the Surviving Corporation will not be converted, exchanged or altered in any manner, but shall remain outstanding shares of the Surviving Corporation.

C. The directors of the Surviving Corporation may, in their discretion, abandon this merger at any time before its effective date.

D. The effective date of this merger shall be the close of business on the date articles of merger relating to this merger are filed as required by law.

2. Shareholder approval of the merger was not required because the Surviving Corporation was the owner of 100% of the outstanding shares of the Merging Corporation, and the Plan of Merger does not provide for any amendment to the articles of incorporation of the Surviving Corporation.

These articles of merger were signed by the corporation on _____.

By: _____

Articles of Merger of

_____

into

_____

These Articles of Merger are submitted by _____,
organized under the laws of _____ (the "Surviving
Corporation") for the purpose of merging _____,
organized under the laws of _____ (the "Merging
Corporation") into the Surviving Corporation.

1. The following Plan of Merger has been duly approved by the boards of directors of the Surviving Corporation and the Merging Corporation:

2. The designation and number of outstanding shares, and the number of votes entitled to be cast by each voting group entitled to vote separately on such Plan as to the Merging Corporation were:

Designation: Shares outstanding: Votes entitled to be cast:

The number of votes cast for such Plan by shareholders of the Merging Corporation was
_____ which was sufficient for approval of the Plan by the shareholders of the Merging Corporation.

3. The designation and number of outstanding shares, and the number of votes entitled to be cast by each voting group entitled to vote separately on such Plan as to the Surviving Corporation were:

<u>Designation:</u>   <u>Shares outstanding:</u>   <u>Votes entitled to be cast:</u>

The number of votes cast for such Plan by shareholders of the Surviving Corporation was _____ which was sufficient for approval of the Plan by the shareholders of the Surviving Corporation.

These articles of merger were signed by the corporation on _____.

By: _____

Stock Ledger

Certificates Issued

Transfer Shares

Cert. No.	No. of Shares	Date Acquired	Shareholder Name and Address	From Whom Transferred	Amount Paid	Date of Transfer	To Whom Transferred	Cert. No. Surrendered	No. of Shares Transferred	Cert. No.

Instructions for Form 2553

(Revised September 1997)

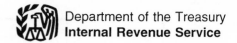

Department of the Treasury
Internal Revenue Service

Election by a Small Business Corporation

Section references are to the Internal Revenue Code unless otherwise noted.

General Instructions

Purpose.— To elect to be an S corporation, a corporation must file Form 2553. The election permits the income of the S corporation to be taxed to the shareholders of the corporation rather than to the corporation itself, except as noted below under **Taxes an S Corporation May Owe.**

Who May Elect.— A corporation may elect to be an S corporation only if it meets all of the following tests:

1. It is a domestic corporation.

2. It has no more than 75 shareholders. A husband and wife (and their estates) are treated as one shareholder for this requirement. All other persons are treated as separate shareholders.

3. Its only shareholders are individuals, estates, certain trusts described in section 1361(c)(2)(A), or, for tax years beginning after 1997, exempt organizations described in section 401(a) or 501(c)(3). Trustees of trusts that want to make the election under section 1361(e)(3) to be an electing small business trust should see Notice 97-12, 1997-3 I.R.B. 11.

Note: *See the instructions for Part III regarding qualified subchapter S trusts.*

4. It has no nonresident alien shareholders.

5. It has only one class of stock (disregarding differences in voting rights). Generally, a corporation is treated as having only one class of stock if all outstanding shares of the corporation's stock confer identical rights to distribution and liquidation proceeds. See Regulations section 1.1361-1(1) for more details.

6. It is not one of the following ineligible corporations:

a. A bank or thrift institution that uses the reserve method of accounting for bad debts under section 585;

b. An insurance company subject to tax under the rules of subchapter L of the Code;

c. A corporation that has elected to be treated as a possessions corporation under section 936; or

d. A domestic international sales corporation (DISC) or former DISC.

7. It has a permitted tax year as required by section 1378 or makes a section 444 election to have a tax year other than a permitted tax year. Section 1378 defines a permitted tax year as a tax year ending December 31, or any other tax year for which the corporation establishes a business purpose to the satisfaction of the IRS. See Part II for details on requesting a fiscal tax year based on a business purpose or on making a section 444 election.

8. Each shareholder consents as explained in the instructions for column K.

See sections 1361, 1362, and 1378 for additional information on the above tests.

An election can be made by a parent S corporation to treat the assets, liabilities, and items of income, deduction, and credit of an eligible wholly-owned subsidiary as those of the parent. For details, see Notice 97-4, 1997-2 I.R.B. 24.

Taxes an S Corporation May Owe.— An S corporation may owe income tax in the following instances:

1. If, at the end of any tax year, the corporation had accumulated earnings and profits, and its passive investment income under section 1362(d)(3) is more than 25% of its gross receipts, the corporation may owe tax on its excess net passive income.

2. A corporation with net recognized built-in gain (as defined in section 1374(d)(2)) may owe tax on its built-in gains.

3. A corporation that claimed investment credit before its first year as an S corporation will be liable for any investment credit recapture tax.

4. A corporation that used the LIFO inventory method for the year immediately preceding its first year as an S corporation may owe an additional tax due to LIFO recapture.

For more details on these taxes, see the Instructions for Form 1120S.

Where To File.— File this election with the Internal Revenue Service Center listed below.

If the corporation's principal business, office, or agency is located in ▼	Use the following Internal Revenue Service Center address ▼
New Jersey, New York (New York City and counties of Nassau, Rockland, Suffolk, and Westchester)	Holtsville, NY 00501
New York (all other counties), Connecticut, Maine, Massachusetts, New Hampshire, Rhode Island, Vermont	Andover, MA 05501
Florida, Georgia, South Carolina	Atlanta, GA 39901
Indiana, Kentucky, Michigan, Ohio, West Virginia	Cincinnati, OH 45999
Kansas, New Mexico, Oklahoma, Texas	Austin, TX 73301
Alaska, Arizona, California (counties of Alpine, Amador, Butte, Calaveras, Colusa, Contra Costa, Del Norte, El Dorado, Glenn, Humboldt, Lake, Lassen, Marin, Mendocino, Modoc, Napa, Nevada, Placer, Plumas, Sacramento, San Joaquin, Shasta, Sierra, Siskiyou, Solano, Sonoma, Sutter, Tehama, Trinity, Yolo, and Yuba), Colorado, Idaho, Montana, Nebraska, Nevada, North Dakota, Oregon, South Dakota, Utah, Washington, Wyoming	Ogden, UT 84201
California (all other counties), Hawaii	Fresno, CA 93888
Illinois, Iowa, Minnesota, Missouri, Wisconsin	Kansas City, MO 64999
Alabama, Arkansas, Louisiana, Mississippi, North Carolina, Tennessee	Memphis, TN 37501
Delaware, District of Columbia, Maryland, Pennsylvania, Virginia	Philadelphia, PA 19255

When To Make the Election.— Complete and file Form 2553 **(a)** at any time before the 16th day of the 3rd month of the tax year, if filed during the tax year the election is to take effect, or **(b)** at any time during the preceding tax year. An election made no later than 2 months and 15 days after the beginning of a tax year that is less than 2½ months long is treated as timely made for that tax year. An election made after the 15th day of the 3rd month but before the end of the tax year is effective for the next year. For example, if a calendar tax year

corporation makes the election in April 1998, it is effective for the corporation's 1999 calendar tax year.

However, an election made after the due date will be accepted as timely filed if the corporation can show that the failure to file on time was due to reasonable cause. To request relief for a late election, the corporation generally must request a private letter ruling and pay a user fee in accordance with Rev. Proc. 97-1, 1997-1 I.R.B. 11 (or its successor). But if the election is filed within 6 months of its due date and the original due date for filing the corporation's initial Form 1120S has not passed, the ruling and user fee requirements do not apply. To request relief in this case, write "FILED PURSUANT TO REV. PROC. 97-40" at the top of page 1 of Form 2553, attach a statement explaining the reason for failing to file the election on time, and file Form 2553 as otherwise instructed. See Rev. Proc. 97-40, 1997-33 I.R.B. 50, for more details.

See Regulations section 1.1362-6(b)(3)(iii) for how to obtain relief for an inadvertent invalid election if the corporation filed a timely election, but one or more shareholders did not file a timely consent.

Acceptance or Nonacceptance of Election.— The service center will notify the corporation if its election is accepted and when it will take effect. The corporation will also be notified if its election is not accepted. The corporation should generally receive a determination on its election within 60 days after it has filed Form 2553. If box Q1 in Part II is checked on page 2, the corporation will receive a ruling letter from the IRS in Washington, DC, that either approves or denies the selected tax year. When box Q1 is checked, it will generally take an additional 90 days for the Form 2553 to be accepted.

Do not file Form 1120S for any tax year before the year the election takes effect. If the corporation is now required to file **Form 1120,** U.S. Corporation Income Tax Return, or any other applicable tax return, continue filing it until the election takes effect.

Care should be exercised to ensure that the IRS receives the election. If the corporation is not notified of acceptance or nonacceptance of its election within 3 months of date of filing (date mailed), or within 6 months if box Q1 is checked, take follow-up action by corresponding with the service center where the corporation filed the election. If the IRS questions whether Form 2553 was filed, an acceptable proof of filing is **(a)** certified or registered mail receipt (timely filed) from the U.S. Postal Service or its equivalent from a designated private delivery service (see Notice 97-26, 1997-17 I.R.B. 6); **(b)** Form 2553 with accepted stamp; **(c)** Form 2553 with stamped IRS received date; or **(d)** IRS letter stating that Form 2553 has been accepted.

End of Election.— Once the election is made, it stays in effect until it is terminated. If the election is terminated in a tax year beginning after 1996, the corporation (or a successor corporation) can make another election on Form 2553 only with IRS consent for any tax year before the 5th tax year after the first tax year in which the termination took effect. See Regulations section 1.1362-5 for more details.

238

Specific Instructions

Part I

Note: *All corporations must complete Part I.*

Name and Address of Corporation.— Enter the true corporate name as stated in the corporate charter or other legal document creating it. If the corporation's mailing address is the same as someone else's, such as a shareholder's, enter "c/o" and this person's name following the name of the corporation. Include the suite, room, or other unit number after the street address. If the Post Office does not deliver to the street address and the corporation has a P.O. box, show the box number instead of the street address. If the corporation changed its name or address after applying for its employer identification number, be sure to check the box in item G of Part I.

Item A. Employer Identification Number (EIN).— If the corporation has applied for an EIN but has not received it, enter "applied for." If the corporation does not have an EIN, it should apply for one on **Form SS-4,** Application for Employer Identification Number. You can order Form SS-4 by calling 1-800-TAX-FORM (1-800-829-3676).

Item D. Effective Date of Election.— Enter the beginning effective date (month, day, year) of the tax year requested for the S corporation. Generally, this will be the beginning date of the tax year for which the ending effective date is required to be shown in item I, Part I. For a new corporation (first year the corporation exists) it will generally be the date required to be shown in item H, Part I. The tax year of a new corporation starts on the date that it has shareholders, acquires assets, or begins doing business, whichever happens first. If the effective date for item D for a newly formed corporation is later than the date in item H, the corporation should file Form 1120 or Form 1120-A for the tax period between these dates.

Column K. Shareholders' Consent Statement.— Each shareholder who owns (or is deemed to own) stock at the time the election is made must consent to the election. If the election is made during the corporation's tax year for which it first takes effect, any person who held stock at any time during the part of that year that occurs before the election is made, must consent to the election, even though the person may have sold or transferred his or her stock before the election is made.

An election made during the first 2½ months of the tax year is effective for the following tax year if any person who held stock in the corporation during the part of the tax year before the election was made, and who did not hold stock at the time the election was made, did not consent to the election.

Each shareholder consents by signing and dating in column K or signing and dating a separate consent statement described below. The following special rules apply in determining who must sign the consent statement.

• If a husband and wife have a community interest in the stock or in the income from it, both must consent.

• Each tenant in common, joint tenant, and tenant by the entirety must consent.

• A minor's consent is made by the minor, legal representative of the minor, or a natural or adoptive parent of the minor if no legal representative has been appointed.

• The consent of an estate is made by the executor or administrator.

• The consent of an electing small business trust is made by the trustee.

• If the stock is owned by a trust (other than an electing small business trust), the deemed owner of the trust must consent. See section 1361(c)(2) for details regarding trusts that are permitted to be shareholders and rules for determining who is the deemed owner.

*Continuation sheet or separate consent statement.—*If you need a continuation sheet or use a separate consent statement, attach it to Form 2553. The separate consent statement must contain the name, address, and EIN of the corporation and the shareholder information requested in columns J through N of Part I. If you want, you may combine all the shareholders' consents in one statement.

Column L.— Enter the number of shares of stock each shareholder owns and the dates the stock was acquired. If the election is made during the corporation's tax year for which it first takes effect, do not list the shares of stock for those shareholders who sold or transferred all of their stock before the election was made. However, these shareholders must still consent to the election for it to be effective for the tax year.

Column M.— Enter the social security number of each shareholder who is an individual. Enter the EIN of each shareholder that is an estate, a qualified trust, or an exempt organization.

Column N.— Enter the month and day that each shareholder's tax year ends. If a shareholder is changing his or her tax year, enter the tax year the shareholder is changing to, and attach an explanation indicating the present tax year and the basis for the change (e.g., automatic revenue procedure or letter ruling request).

Signature.— Form 2553 must be signed by the president, treasurer, assistant treasurer, chief accounting officer, or other corporate officer (such as tax officer) authorized to sign.

Part II

Complete Part II if you selected a tax year ending on any date other than December 31 (other than a 52-53-week tax year ending with reference to the month of December).

Box P1.— Attach a statement showing separately for each month the amount of gross receipts for the most recent 47 months as required by section 4.03(3) of Rev. Proc. 87-32, 1987-2 C.B. 396. A corporation that does not have a 47-month period of gross receipts cannot establish a natural business year under section 4.01(1).

Box Q1.— For examples of an acceptable business purpose for requesting a fiscal tax year, see Rev. Rul. 87-57, 1987-2 C.B. 117.

In addition to a statement showing the business purpose for the requested fiscal year, you must attach the other information necessary to meet the ruling request requirements of Rev. Proc. 97-1 (or its successor). Also attach a statement that shows separately the amount of gross receipts from sales or services (and inventory costs, if applicable) for each of the 36 months preceding the effective date of the election to be an S corporation. If the corporation has been in existence for fewer than 36 months, submit figures for the period of existence.

If you check box Q1, you will be charged a $250 user fee (subject to change). Do not pay the fee when filing Form 2553. The service center will send Form 2553 to the IRS in Washington, DC, who, in turn, will notify the corporation that the fee is due.

Box Q2.— If the corporation makes a back-up section 444 election for which it is qualified, then the election will take effect in the event the business purpose request is not approved. In some cases, the tax year requested under the back-up section 444 election may be different than the tax year requested under business purpose. See **Form 8716,** Election To Have a Tax Year Other Than a Required Tax Year, for details on making a back-up section 444 election.

Boxes Q2 and R2.— If the corporation is not qualified to make the section 444 election after making the item Q2 back-up section 444 election or indicating its intention to make the election in item R1, and therefore it later files a calendar year return, it should write "Section 444 Election Not Made" in the top left corner of the first calendar year Form 1120S it files.

Part III

Certain qualified subchapter S trusts (QSSTs) may make the QSST election required by section 1361(d)(2) in Part III. Part III may be used to make the QSST election only if corporate stock has been transferred to the trust on or before the date on which the corporation makes its election to be an S corporation. However, a statement can be used instead of Part III to make the election.

Note: *Use Part III only if you make the election in Part I (i.e., Form 2553 cannot be filed with only Part III completed).*

The deemed owner of the QSST must also consent to the S corporation election in column K, page 1, of Form 2553. See section 1361 (c)(2).

Paperwork Reduction Act Notice.— We ask for the information on this form to carry out the Internal Revenue laws of the United States. You are required to give us the information. We need it to ensure that you are complying with these laws and to allow us to figure and collect the right amount of tax.

You are not required to provide the information requested on a form that is subject to the Paperwork Reduction Act unless the form displays a valid OMB control number. Books or records relating to a form or its instructions must be retained as long as their contents may become material in the administration of any Internal Revenue law. Generally, tax returns and return information are confidential, as required by section 6103.

The time needed to complete and file this form will depend on individual circumstances. The estimated average time is:

Recordkeeping .... 6 hr., 28 min.

Learning about the
law or the form................................... 3 hr., 41 min.

Preparing, copying,
assembling, and sending
the form to the IRS .... 3 hr., 56 min.

If you have comments concerning the accuracy of these time estimates or suggestions for making this form simpler, we would be happy to hear from you. You can write to the Tax Forms Committee, Western Area Distribution Center, Rancho Cordova, CA 95743-0001. **DO NOT** send the form to this address. Instead, see **Where To File** on page 1.

Form **2553**
(Rev. September 1997)

Department of the Treasury
Internal Revenue Service

Election by a Small Business Corporation

(Under section 1362 of the Internal Revenue Code)

▶ For Paperwork Reduction Act Notice, see page 2 of instructions.

▶ See separate instructions.

OMB No. 1545-0146

Notes:
1. This election to be an S corporation can be accepted only if all the tests are met under **Who May Elect** on page 1 of the instructions; all signatures in Parts I and III are originals (no photocopies); and the exact name and address of the corporation and other required form information are provided.

2. Do not file **Form 1120S**, U.S. Income Tax Return for an S Corporation, for any tax year before the year the election takes effect.

3. If the corporation was in existence before the effective date of this election, see **Taxes an S Corporation May Owe** on page 1 of the instructions.

Part I   Election Information

Please Type or Print

Name of corporation (see instructions)	**A** Employer identification number
Number, street, and room or suite no. (If a P.O. box, see instructions.)	**B** Date incorporated
City or town, state, and ZIP code	**C** State of incorporation

D Election is to be effective for tax year beginning (month, day, year) . . . . ▶   /   /

E Name and title of officer or legal representative who the IRS may call for more information

F Telephone number of officer or legal representative

(   )

G If the corporation changed its name or address after applying for the EIN shown in **A** above, check this box . . . . ▶ ☐

H If this election takes effect for the first tax year the corporation exists, enter month, day, and year of the **earliest** of the following: (1) date the corporation first had shareholders, (2) date the corporation first had assets, or (3) date the corporation began doing business . . . . ▶   /   /

I Selected tax year: Annual return will be filed for tax year ending (month and day) ▶ -

If the tax year ends on any date other than December 31, except for an automatic 52-53-week tax year ending with reference to the month of December, you **must** complete Part II on the back. If the date you enter is the ending date of an automatic 52-53-week tax year, write "52-53-week year" to the right of the date. See Temporary Regulations section 1.441-2T(e)(3).

J Name and address of each shareholder; shareholder's spouse having a community property interest in the corporation's stock; and each tenant in common, joint tenant, and tenant by the entirety. (A husband and wife (and their estates) are counted as one shareholder in determining the number of shareholders without regard to the manner in which the stock is owned.)	**K** Shareholders' Consent Statement. Under penalties of perjury, we declare that we consent to the election of the above-named corporation to be an S corporation under section 1362(a) and that we have examined this consent statement, including accompanying schedules and statements, and to the best of our knowledge and belief, it is true, correct, and complete. We understand our consent is binding and may not be withdrawn after the corporation has made a valid election. (Shareholders sign and date below.)		**L** Stock owned		**M** Social security number or employer identification number (see instructions)	**N** Share-holder's tax year ends (month and day)
	Signature	Date	Number of shares	Dates acquired		

Under penalties of perjury, I declare that I have examined this election, including accompanying schedules and statements, and to the best of my knowledge and belief, it is true, correct, and complete.

Signature of officer ▶   Title ▶   Date ▶

See Parts II and III on back.   Cat. No. 18629R   Form **2553** (Rev. 9-97)

Part II   **Selection of Fiscal Tax Year** (All corporations using this part must complete item O and item P, Q, or R.)

O   Check the applicable box to indicate whether the corporation is:

   1. ☐ A new corporation adopting the tax year entered in item I, Part I.

   2. ☐ An existing corporation retaining the tax year entered in item I, Part I.

   3. ☐ An existing corporation changing to the tax year entered in item I, Part I.

P   Complete item P if the corporation is using the expeditious approval provisions of Rev. Proc. 87-32, 1987-2 C.B. 396, to request **(1)** a natural business year (as defined in section 4.01(1) of Rev. Proc. 87-32) or **(2)** a year that satisfies the ownership tax year test in section 4.01(2) of Rev. Proc. 87-32. Check the applicable box below to indicate the representation statement the corporation is making as required under section 4 of Rev. Proc. 87-32.

   1. Natural Business Year ▶ ☐ I represent that the corporation is retaining or changing to a tax year that coincides with its natural business year as defined in section 4.01(1) of Rev. Proc. 87-32 and as verified by its satisfaction of the requirements of section 4.02(1) of Rev. Proc. 87-32. In addition, if the corporation is changing to a natural business year as defined in section 4.01(1), I further represent that such tax year results in less deferral of income to the owners than the corporation's present tax year. I also represent that the corporation is not described in section 3.01(2) of Rev. Proc. 87-32. (See instructions for additional information that must be attached.)

   2. Ownership Tax Year ▶ ☐ I represent that shareholders holding more than half of the shares of the stock (as of the first day of the tax year to which the request relates) of the corporation have the same tax year or are concurrently changing to the tax year that the corporation adopts, retains, or changes to per item I, Part I. I also represent that the corporation is not described in section 3.01(2) of Rev. Proc. 87-32.

Note: *If you do not use item P and the corporation wants a fiscal tax year, complete either item Q or R below. Item Q is used to request a fiscal tax year based on a business purpose and to make a back-up section 444 election. Item R is used to make a regular section 444 election.*

Q   Business Purpose—To request a fiscal tax year based on a business purpose, you must check box Q1 and pay a user fee. See instructions for details. You may also check box Q2 and/or box Q3.

   1. Check here ▶ ☐ if the fiscal year entered in item I, Part I, is requested under the provisions of section 6.03 of Rev. Proc. 87-32. Attach to Form 2553 a statement showing the business purpose for the requested fiscal year. See instructions for additional information that must be attached.

   2. Check here ▶ ☐ to show that the corporation intends to make a back-up section 444 election in the event the corporation's business purpose request is not approved by the IRS. (See instructions for more information.)

   3. Check here ▶ ☐ to show that the corporation agrees to adopt or change to a tax year ending December 31 if necessary for the IRS to accept this election for S corporation status in the event (1) the corporation's business purpose request is not approved and the corporation makes a back-up section 444 election, but is ultimately not qualified to make a section 444 election, or (2) the corporation's business purpose request is not approved and the corporation did not make a back-up section 444 election.

R   Section 444 Election—To make a section 444 election, you must check box R1 and you may also check box R2.

   1. Check here ▶ ☐ to show the corporation will make, if qualified, a section 444 election to have the fiscal tax year shown in item I, Part I. To make the election, you must complete **Form 8716,** Election To Have a Tax Year Other Than a Required Tax Year, and either attach it to Form 2553 or file it separately.

   2. Check here ▶ ☐ to show that the corporation agrees to adopt or change to a tax year ending December 31 if necessary for the IRS to accept this election for S corporation status in the event the corporation is ultimately not qualified to make a section 444 election.

Part III   **Qualified Subchapter S Trust (QSST) Election Under Section 1361(d)(2)***

Income beneficiary's name and address	Social security number
Trust's name and address	Employer identification number

Date on which stock of the corporation was transferred to the trust (month, day, year) . . . . ▶   /   /

In order for the trust named above to be a QSST and thus a qualifying shareholder of the S corporation for which this Form 2553 is filed, I hereby make the election under section 1361(d)(2). Under penalties of perjury, I certify that the trust meets the definitional requirements of section 1361(d)(3) and that all other information provided in Part III is true, correct, and complete.

_____   _____
Signature of income beneficiary or signature and title of legal representative or other qualified person making the election   Date

*Use Part III to make the QSST election only if stock of the corporation has been transferred to the trust on or before the date on which the corporation makes its election to be an S corporation. The QSST election must be made and filed separately if stock of the corporation is transferred to the trust after the date on which the corporation makes the S election.

Noncompetition and Nondisclosure Agreement

This agreement is made between_____
(the "Employee") and _____ (the "Corporation").
The Employee agrees to the terms of this agreement in consideration of the Employee's contin-
ued employment by the Corporation and additional consideration consisting of
_____

_____, which the Employee acknowledges is
consideration paid by the Corporation over and above the consideration due to the Employee
pursuant to his or her usual terms of employment. The Employee also acknowledges the receipt
and sufficiency of such consideration to support his or her promises made in this agreement.

1.   The Employee agrees that upon termination of employment for any reason, he or
she will not enter into competition with the Corporation, its successors or assigns, in the area and
for the period of time stated below.

2.   For purposes of this agreement, the term "competition" shall mean any activity of
the Employee consisting of or related to (a) soliciting orders for any product or service competi-
tive with the Corporation, (b) contracting, for the purpose of soliciting business, any customer,
client or account of the Corporation in existence during the term of his or her employment by
the Corporation, (c) disclosing confidential information of the Corporation, including but not
limited to trade secrets, customer lists, supplier lists and prices, and pricing schedules, or without
in any way limiting the foregoing, (d):

Any such activity shall be considered "competition" whether undertaken directly or indirectly, as
an owner, officer, director, employee, consultant, stockholder, partner or in any other relationship
with a competing business.

3.   The period of time referred to in paragraph 1 above shall be _____ months
following the termination of the Employee's employment by the Corporation, and the area
referred to in paragraph 1 above shall be limited to the following:

4.   Violation of this agreement by the Employee will entitle the Corporation to an
injunction to prevent such competition or disclosure, with posting of any bond by the
Corporation; and will entitle the Corporation to other legal remedies, including attorneys fees and
costs.

5.   This agreement may not be modified except in writing signed by both parties.

This agreement was executed by the Employee and by the Corporation by authority of its
Board of Directors on _____, _____.

Dated:_____   Dated:_____

Employee: Corporation:

_____   By:_____

Assignment of Assets

This agreement is made this _____ day of _____, _____, by and between _____ ("Shareholder") and _____, a _____ corporation ("Corporation"), who agree as follows:

    1.   The Shareholder hereby transfers and assigns the assets listed on the attached Exhibit "A" to the Corporation.

    2.   In consideration for said transfer and assignment of assets, the Corporation shall issued to the Shareholder _____ shares of _____ stock in the Corporation, with a par value of $_____ per share.

Shareholder: Corporation:

_____   By:_____

Articles of Amendment of

_____

The Articles of Incorporation of _____

_____are hereby amended as follows:

The date of these Articles of Amendment is_____.

By:_____

Certification of Secretary of

_____

I HEREBY CERTIFY that I am the Corporate Secretary of _____
_____; that I am the custodian of the official corporate
records of all stock ownership; and that, as of this date, there is a total of _____
shares of capital stock of the corporation issued and outstanding.

Signed and the seal of the Corporation affixed, _____, _____.

_____

Secretary

Certification of Secretary of

_____

      I HEREBY CERTIFY that I am the Corporate Secretary of _____

_____, and that the attached (describe documents):

are true and accurate copies of the records and documents of the corporation.

      Signed and the seal of the Corporation affixed, _____, _____.

_____
Secretary

STATE OF
COUNTY OF

      On _____, _____, there personally appeared before me, _____, who, being duly sworn, deposed and said that he/she is the Secretary of _____, and that the facts stated in the above Affidavit are true.

_____
Notary Public
My Commission Expires:

INDEX

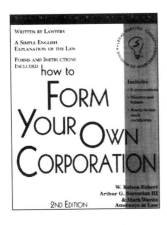  

SPHINX® PUBLISHING'S NATIONAL TITLES
Valid in All 50 States

LEGAL SURVIVAL IN BUSINESS

How to Form a Limited Liability Company (April)	$19.95
How to Form Your Own Corporation (2E)	$19.95
How to Form Your Own Partnership	$19.95
How to Register Your Own Copyright (2E)	$19.95
How to Register Your Own Trademark (2E)	$19.95
Most Valuable Business Legal Forms You'll Ever Need (2E)	$19.95
Most Valuable Corporate Forms You'll Ever Need (2E)	$24.95
Software Law (with diskette)	$29.95

LEGAL SURVIVAL IN COURT

Crime Victim's Guide to Justice	$19.95
Debtors' Rights (3E)	$12.95
Defend Yourself against Criminal Charges	$19.95
Grandparents' Rights (2E)	$19.95
Help Your Lawyer Win Your Case	$12.95
Jurors' Rights (2E)	$9.95
Legal Malpractice and Other Claims against Your Lawyer (2E) (June)	$18.95
Legal Research Made Easy (2E)	$14.95
Simple Ways to Protect Yourself from Lawsuits	$24.95
Victims' Rights	$12.95
Winning Your Personal Injury Claim	$19.95

LEGAL SURVIVAL IN REAL ESTATE

How to Buy a Condominium or Townhome	$16.95
How to Negotiate Real Estate Contracts (3E)	$16.95
How to Negotiate Real Estate Leases (3E)	$16.95
Successful Real Estate Brokerage Management	$19.95

LEGAL SURVIVAL IN PERSONAL AFFAIRS

How to File Your Own Bankruptcy (4E)	$19.95
How to File Your Own Divorce (3E)	$19.95
How to Make Your Own Will	$12.95
How to Write Your Own Living Will	$9.95
How to Write Your Own Premarital Agreement (2E)	$19.95
How to Win Your Unemployment Compensation Claim	$19.95
Living Trusts and Simple Ways to Avoid Probate (2E)	$19.95
Neighbors' Rights	$12.95
The Power of Attorney Handbook (3E)	$19.95
Simple Ways to Protect Yourself from Lawsuits	$24.95
Social Security Benefits Handbook (2E)	$14.95
Unmarried Parents' Rights	$19.95
U.S.A. Immigration Guide (3E)	$19.95
Guia de Inmigracion a Estados Unidos (2E) (May)	$19.95

Legal Survival Guides are directly available from Sourcebooks, Inc., or from your local bookstores.

For credit card orders call 1–800–43–BRIGHT, write P.O. Box 372, Naperville, IL 60566,
or fax 630-961-2168

LEGAL SURVIVAL GUIDES™ STATE TITLES
Up-to-date for Your State

CALIFORNIA

How to File for Divorce in CA	$19.95
How to Make a CA Will	$12.95
How to Start a Business in CA	$16.95
How to Win in Small Claims Court in CA	$14.95
Landlords' Rights and Duties in CA	$19.95
CA Power of Attorney Handbook	$19.95

FLORIDA

Florida Power of Attorney Handbook	$9.95
How to Change Your Name in FL (3E)	$14.95
How to File a FL Construction Lien (2E)	$19.95
How to File a Guardianship in FL	$19.95
How to File for Divorce in FL (4E)	$21.95
How to Form a Nonprofit Corp in FL (3E)	$19.95
How to Form a Corporation in FL (4E)	$19.95
How to Make a FL Will (5E)	$12.95
How to Modify Your FL Divorce Judgement (3E)	$22.95
How to Probate an Estate in FL (2E)	$24.95
How to Start a Business in FL (4E)	$16.95
How to Win in Small Claims Court in FL (6E)	$14.95
Land Trusts in FL (5E)	$24.95
Landlords' Rights and Duties in FL (7E)	$19.95
Women's Legal Rights in FL	$19.95

GEORGIA

How to File for Divorce in GA (2E)	$19.95
How to Make a GA Will (2E)	$9.95
How to Start and Run a GA Business (2E)	$18.95

ILLINOIS

How to File for Divorce in IL	$19.95
How to Make an IL Will	$9.95
How to Start a Business in IL	$16.95

MASSACHUSETTS

How to File for Divorce in MA (2E)	$19.95
How to Make a MA Will	$9.95
How to Probate an Estate in MA	$19.95
How to Start a Business in MA	$16.95
Landlords' Rights and Duties in MA	$19.95

MICHIGAN

How to File for Divorce in MI	$19.95
How to Make a MI Will	$9.95
How to Start a Business in MI	$16.95

MINNESOTA

How to File for Divorce in MN	$19.95
How to Form a Simple Corporation in MN	$19.95
How to Make a MN Will	$9.95
How to Start a Business in MN	$16.95

NEW YORK

How to File for Divorce in NY	$19.95
How to Make a NY Will	$12.95
How to Start a Business in NY	$16.95
How to Win in Small Claims Court in NY	$14.95
Landlords' Rights and Duties in NY	$19.95
New York Power of Attorney Handbook	$12.95

NORTH CAROLINA

How to File for Divorce in NC (2E)	$19.95
How to Make a NC Will (2E)	$9.95
How to Start a Business in NC	$16.95

PENNSYLVANIA

How to File for Divorce in PA	$19.95
How to Make a PA Will	$12.95
How to Start a Business in PA	$16.95
Landlords' Rights and Duties in PA	$19.95

TEXAS

How to File for Divorce in TX (2E)	$19.95
How to Form a Simple Corporation in TX	$19.95
How to Make a TX Will	$9.95
How to Probate an Estate in TX	$19.95
How to Start a Business in TX	$16.95
How to Win in Small Claims Court in TX	$14.95
Landlords' Rights and Duties in TX	$19.95

Legal Survival Guides are directly available from the publisher, or from your local bookstores.

For credit card orders call 1–800–43–BRIGHT, write P.O. Box 372, Naperville, IL 60566,
or fax 630-961-2168

SPHINX® PUBLISHING ORDER FORM

BILL TO:

SHIP TO:

Phone #	Terms	F.O.B. Chicago, IL	Ship Date

Charge my: ☐ VISA ☐ MasterCard ☐ American Express

☐ **Money Order or Personal Check**

Credit Card Number

Expiration Date

Qty	ISBN	Title	Retail	Ext.
		SPHINX PUBLISHING NATIONAL TITLES		
	1-57071-166-6	Crime Victim's Guide to Justice	$19.95	
	1-57071-342-1	Debtors' Rights (3E)	$12.95	
	1-57071-162-3	Defend Yourself against Criminal Charges	$19.95	
	1-57248-082-3	Grandparents' Rights (2E)	$19.95	
	1-57248-087-4	Guia de Inmigracion a Estados Unidos (2E) (May)	$19.95	
	1-57248-021-1	Help Your Lawyer Win Your Case	$12.95	
	1-57071-164-X	How to Buy a Condominium or Townhome	$16.95	
	1-57071-223-9	How to File Your Own Bankruptcy (4E)	$19.95	
	1-57071-224-7	How to File Your Own Divorce (3E)	$19.95	
	1-57248-083-1	How to Form a Limited Liability Company (April)	$19.95	
	1-57071-227-1	How to Form Your Own Corporation (2E)	$19.95	
	1-57071-343-X	How to Form Your Own Partnership	$19.95	
	1-57071-228-X	How to Make Your Own Will	$12.95	
	1-57071-331-6	How to Negotiate Real Estate Contracts (3E)	$16.95	
	1-57071-332-4	How to Negotiate Real Estate Leases (3E)	$16.95	
	1-57071-225-5	How to Register Your Own Copyright (2E)	$19.95	
	1-57071-226-3	How to Register Your Own Trademark (2E)	$19.95	
	1-57071-349-9	How to Win Your Unemployment Compensation Claim	$19.95	
	1-57071-167-4	How to Write Your Own Living Will	$9.95	
	1-57071-344-8	How to Write Your Own Premarital Agreement (2E)	$19.95	
	1-57071-333-2	Jurors' Rights (2E)	$9.95	
	1-57248-090-4	Legal Malpractice and Other Claims against...(2E) (June)	$18.95	
	1-57071-400-2	Legal Research Made Easy (2E)	$14.95	
	1-57071-336-7	Living Trusts and Simple Ways to Avoid Probate (2E)	$19.95	
	1-57071-345-6	Most Valuable Bus. Legal Forms You'll Ever Need (2E)	$19.95	
	1-57071-346-4	Most Valuable Corporate Forms You'll Ever Need (2E)	$24.95	

Qty	ISBN	Title	Retail	Ext.
	1-57248-089-0	Neighbors' Rights	$12.95	
	1-57071-348-0	The Power of Attorney Handbook (3E)	$19.95	
	1-57248-020-3	Simple Ways to Protect Yourself from Lawsuits	$24.95	
	1-57071-337-5	Social Security Benefits Handbook (2E)	$14.95	
	1-57071-163-1	Software Law (w/diskette)	$29.95	
	0-913825-86-7	Successful Real Estate Brokerage Mgmt.	$19.95	
	1-57071-399-5	Unmarried Parents' Rights	$19.95	
	1-57071-354-5	U.S.A. Immigration Guide (3E)	$19.95	
	0-913825-82-4	Victims' Rights	$12.95	
	1-57071-165-8	Winning Your Personal Injury Claim	$19.95	
		CALIFORNIA TITLES		
	1-57071-360-X	CA Power of Attorney Handbook	$12.95	
	1-57071-355-3	How to File for Divorce in CA	$19.95	
	1-57071-356-1	How to Make a CA Will	$12.95	
	1-57071-408-8	How to Probate an Estate in CA (April)	$19.95	
	1-57071-357-X	How to Start a Business in CA	$16.95	
	1-57071-358-8	How to Win in Small Claims Court in CA	$14.95	
	1-57071-359-6	Landlords' Rights and Duties in CA	$19.95	
		FLORIDA TITLES		
	1-57071-363-4	Florida Power of Attorney Handbook (2E)	$12.95	
	1-57248-093-9	How to File for Divorce in FL (6E) (July)	$21.95	
	1-57248-086-6	How to Form a Limited Liability Co. in FL (April)	$19.95	
	1-57071-401-0	How to Form a Partnership in FL	$19.95	
	1-57071-380-4	How to Form a Corporation in FL (4E)	$19.95	
	1-57071-361-8	How to Make a FL Will (5E)	$12.95	
	1-57248-088-2	How to Modify Your FL Divorce Judgement (4E)(May)	$22.95	
		Form Continued on Following Page	**SUBTOTAL**	

To order, call Sourcebooks at 1-800-43-BRIGHT or FAX (630)961-2168 (Bookstores, libraries, wholesalers—please call for discount)

SPHINX® PUBLISHING ORDER FORM

Qty	ISBN	Title	Retail	Ext.
		FLORIDA TITLES (CONT'D)		
_____	1-57071-364-2	How to Probate an Estate in FL (3E)	$24.95	_____
_____	1-57248-081-5	How to Start a Business in FL (5E) (March)	$16.95	_____
_____	1-57071-362-6	How to Win in Small Claims Court in FL (6E)	$14.95	_____
_____	1-57071-335-9	Landlords' Rights and Duties in FL (7E)	$19.95	_____
_____	1-57071-334-0	Land Trusts in FL (5E)	$24.95	_____
_____	0-913825-73-5	Women's Legal Rights in FL	$19.95	_____
		GEORGIA TITLES		
_____	1-57071-376-6	How to File for Divorce in GA (3E)	$19.95	_____
_____	1-57248-075-0	How to Make a GA Will (3E)	$12.95	_____
_____	1-57248-076-9	How to Start a Business in Georgia (3E)	$16.95	_____
		ILLINOIS TITLES		
_____	1-57071-405-3	How to File for Divorce in IL (2E)	$19.95	_____
_____	1-57071-415-0	How to Make an IL Will (2E)	$12.95	_____
_____	1-57071-416-9	How to Start a Business in IL (2E)	$16.95	_____
_____	1-57248-078-5	Landlords' Rights & Duties in IL (February)	$19.95	_____
		MASSACHUSETTS TITLES		
_____	1-57071-329-4	How to File for Divorce in MA (2E)	$19.95	_____
_____	1-57248-050-5	How to Make a MA Will	$9.95	_____
_____	1-57248-053-X	How to Probate an Estate in MA	$19.95	_____
_____	1-57248-054-8	How to Start a Business in MA	$16.95	_____
_____	1-57248-055-6	Landlords' Rights and Duties in MA	$19.95	_____
		MICHIGAN TITLES		
_____	1-57071-409-6	How to File for Divorce in MI (2E)	$19.95	_____
_____	1-57248-077-7	How to Make a MI Will (2E)	$12.95	_____
_____	1-57071-407-X	How to Start a Business in MI (2E)	$16.95	_____
		MINNESOTA TITLES		
_____	1-57248-039-4	How to File for Divorce in MN	$19.95	_____
_____	1-57248-040-8	How to Form a Simple Corporation in MN	$19.95	_____
_____	1-57248-037-8	How to Make a MN Will	$9.95	_____
_____	1-57248-038-6	How to Start a Business in MN	$16.95	_____
		NEW YORK TITLES		

Qty	ISBN	Title	Retail	Ext.
_____	1-57071-184-4	How to File for Divorce in NY (March)	$19.95	_____
_____	1-57248-095-5	How to Make a NY Will (2E)	$12.95	_____
_____	1-57071-185-2	How to Start a Business in NY	$16.95	_____
_____	1-57071-187-9	How to Win in Small Claims Court in NY	$14.95	_____
_____	1-57071-186-0	Landlords' Rights and Duties in NY (March)	$19.95	_____
_____	1-57071-188-7	New York Power of Attorney Handbook	$19.95	_____
		NORTH CAROLINA TITLES		
_____	1-57071-326-X	How to File for Divorce in NC (2E)	$19.95	_____
_____	1-57071-327-8	How to Make a NC Will (2E)	$12.95	_____
_____	1-57248-096-3	How to Start a Business in NC (2E)	$16.95	_____
_____	1-57248-091-2	Landlords' Rights & Duties in NC (June)	$19.95	_____
		PENNSYLVANIA TITLES		
_____	1-57071-177-1	How to File for Divorce in PA	$19.95	_____
_____	1-57248-094-7	How to Make a PA Will (2E)	$12.95	_____
_____	1-57071-178-X	How to Start a Business in PA	$16.95	_____
_____	1-57071-179-8	Landlords' Rights and Duties in PA (June)	$19.95	_____
		TEXAS TITLES		
_____	1-57071-330-8	How to File for Divorce in TX (2E)	$19.95	_____
_____	1-57248-009-2	How to Form a Simple Corporation in TX	$19.95	_____
_____	1-57071-417-7	How to Make a TX Will (2E)	$12.95	_____
_____	1-57071-418-5	How to Probate an Estate in TX (2E)	$19.95	_____
_____	1-57071-365-0	How to Start a Business in TX (2E)	$16.95	_____
_____	1-57248-012-2	How to Win in Small Claims Court in TX	$14.95	_____
_____	1-57248-011-4	Landlords' Rights and Duties in TX	$19.95	_____

SUBTOTAL THIS PAGE _____

SUBTOTAL PREVIOUS PAGE _____

Illinois residents add 6.75% sales tax

Florida residents add 6% state sales tax plus applicable discretionary surtax _____

Shipping— $4.00 for 1st book, $1.00 each additional _____

TOTAL _____